What Others Are Saying About
Wendy De Rosa and *Expanding Your Heart*:

"Wendy De Rosa has studied sacred wisdom traditions for many years, and she has distilled that wisdom through the power of her own direct experience, which gives power and authenticity to her work. She teaches clarity and love from her experience, and because of that, the power of her heart is present. She shares deep healing wisdom throughout this book in non-dogmatic ways that will help others to get in touch with their own truth, feelings, and Spirit! In person, Wendy radiates warmth, loving e⟨   ⟩ wisdom, and she has channeled that into this book. For st⟨   ⟩ are sincerely interested in inner healing, finding their voi⟨   ⟩ dging Eastern wisdom with our Western modern reality—⟨   ⟩ nd this book. May all beings be happy and free."

— Saul Da⟨   ⟩ Yoga Teacher, Activist, Musician

"Wendy is a gifted healer ⟨   ⟩ ɘ to help us all break through the blocks and connect to the ⟨   ⟩ ɾ Self we need to create our best life. Her practical information is simply divine!"

— Kara Sundlun, News Anchor, Co-Host of
Better Connecticut, WFSB-TV

"I don't do these things, go to spiritual awakenings, but I did go to Wendy's, and she was fantastic. If you're open to it, Wendy can provide some very useful tools."

— Scot Haney, WFSB, Channel 3 Eyewitness News

"This book will change your life. Wendy helps you see that your life challenges are the greatest opening of your life. The Four Stages are brilliant! You will never see your life challenges the same way again as you search for your truth."

— Nicole Gabriel, Author of *Finding Your Inner Truth*

"A true game-changer! *Expanding Your Heart: Awakening Through Four Stages of a Spiritual Opening* speaks to the tremendous consciousness shift that is happening on the planet right now. We are not meant to live the pain of our past; we are meant to see that we are here to live our fullest selves. Wendy De Rosa provides the tools, healing, and road map to support this process."

— Patrick Snow, International Best-Selling Author of *Creating Your Own Destiny* and *The Affluent Entrepreneur*

"Filled with intuitive wisdom, this book takes you on a powerful journey of self-exploration to help overcome personal challenges and to become more conscious of how you live your life."

— Susan Friedmann, CSP, International Best-Selling Author of *Riches in Niches: How to Make it BIG in a small Market*

"If we are to heal the planet, our hearts must open. *Expanding Your Heart* is an intuitive guide to the stages of heart awakening. Each stage recognized is a step on the journey home to greater fulfillment, creativity, kindness, compassion, and a fulfilled and happy life. Our planetary and human existence depends on it!"

— Jeanie Manchester, Yogini, Founder of Shakti Rise Immersion— Women Leaders on the Rise for Planetary Healing

"Wendy has a special talent for tapping into the power of intuition to help people deepen their connections, open their hearts, and discover their life's purpose. This book shows you how to recognize your own spiritual awakenings, which often come disguised as painful and challenging circumstances. When viewed from a different perspective, these experiences can become our best teachers."

— Tracy Maxwell, Speaker & Healing Coach, Author of *Being Single With Cancer*

"Wendy has been instrumental in my emotional and spiritual healing and growth. As a psychotherapist, I have worked on myself for years, and the spiritual perspective and connection that Wendy provides has added a new dimension not only to my own growth, but in how I have also taken her teachings and integrated them into my own work. I am forever grateful for Wendy and all she has to offer."

— Dr. Dori Gatter, LPC, Founder of the Temple of Success Coaching and Therapy Program and DrDoriGatter.com

"Too often, trauma happens and then becomes the defining moment of collapse in life. Wendy De Rosa's Four Stages of a Spiritual Opening are a simply understood, yet powerful hand-holding guide for not only staying open, but blossoming into the next level of awareness— awareness leading to authentic happiness and fulfillment. De Rosa's book is a priceless gift to all who have searched and yearned for a more meaningful life."

— Tamara Star, Internationally Recognized Author, Coach, and Founder of DailyTransformations.com and the 40 Day Personal Reboot for Women

"Wendy's stages of heart opening and transformation are not only brilliant, but so desperately needed in a world where many are struggling for spiritual grounding. These stages bring light to real-life emotions, heartaches, life transitions, and joyful shifts. Follow Wendy's guidance and you will be amazed at the power of your own heart's healing!"

— Cynthia Stadd, Food Relationship Expert and Speaker

"Wendy's book will assist you in navigating your spiritual heart and understanding that sometimes your greatest pain can afford your greatest opportunity. May your journey into your heart allow you to heal so you may fully embody, express, and manifest your Spirit out and into the world."

— Tina Walsh, Therapist, Yoga Teacher, Healer

EXPANDING YOUR HEART

AWAKENING THROUGH
FOUR STAGES OF A
SPIRITUAL OPENING

WENDY DE ROSA

AVIVA
PUBLISHING
New York

EXPANDING YOUR HEART
AWAKENING THROUGH FOUR STAGES OF A SPIRITUAL OPENING

Copyright © 2015 by Wendy De Rosa. All rights reserved.

Published by:
Aviva Publishing
Lake Placid, NY
(518) 523-1320 www.AvivaPubs.com

Wendy De Rosa
www.SchoolofIntuitiveStudies.com

ISBN: 978-1-943164-10-3

Library of Congress Control Number: 2015905550

Editor: Tyler Tichelaar
Content Editor: Bridget Keller
Cover Designer: Ivan Junge, Bison Design Group
Book Layout: NicoleGabriel, www.AngelDogProductions.com
Author Photo: Fabrizio Darold

Every attempt has been made to source properly all quotes.

Printed in the United States of America

First Edition

This book is dedicated to:

James, Isaac, and Lucciana, who have
opened my heart more than I could have dreamed.

To all those who have walked this healing path with me.

To those who would benefit from having a guide
through the process of struggle, chaos, healing,
and the expansion of the true self.

May you know your own light in the
face of your courageous journey.

ACKNOWLEDGMENTS

I wish to thank the following people for their support and contributions to this book:

Ellen De Rosa, Vincent De Rosa, David De Rosa, Holly and Jason Walejeski, Krista De Rosa, Greg and Renee De Rosa, Tim De Rosa, Ron De Rosa, Cassandra De Rosa, James Flores, Isaac and Lucciana, Bridget Keller, Ashley Henderson, Saul David Raye, Cynthia Stadd, Julie Saffir, Dori Gatter, Tamara Star, Carmen Cook, Beth DeGennaro, Kathy Feinerman, Tracy Maxwell, Trish Mitchell, Susie Romak, Patrick Snow, and all my clients throughout the years who have taught me to be the healer I am today.

Thank you for sharing your lives and stories with me.

CONTENTS

Preface:

HOW TO USE THIS BOOK

The Four Stages you will learn about in this book are meant to help you gain spiritual strength in relation to the difficult experiences that happen to every single person on this planet, and to see such experiences as springboards for expansion, NOT as catalogs of failure. We are evolving in consciousness, and for that reason, spiritual teachers and leaders are spreading their teachings to help others have manageable frameworks for living life on Earth as embodied souls. You are a spiritually progressing soul, and as such, you will always have the ability to transform pain to peace, fear to love, and confusion to joy. This book will take you deep into the spiritual understanding of difficult situations—and into healing.

Use this book as a tool for healing. The meditations, Healing Guide, and questions in this book are designed to help you heal. As you relate the Four Stages to your own personal life, you will soon realize that you are not alone in your experience. I am here to support you by offering guidelines and questions at the end of each chapter that you can share with your friends, loved ones, and peers as you explore the Four Stages in your life.

In addition, I encourage you to join or form book club groups to meet and discuss your experience with this book as it relates to your life. Healing can happen through connection to others on a similar journey. In the back of the book are book club guidelines to follow. The reason I am suggesting guidelines is because transformation is an intense experience. Support systems are necessary during a process. Although a book club is a support system, not every book club leader or participant is qualified to manage a deep personal process; therefore, I recommend also seeking a therapist or qualified practitioner to support your process as needed. In addition to the guidelines in this book, you can visit my website to learn more about book clubs: www.SchoolofIntuitiveStudies.com.

Wendy:
Isaac, what does Expanding Your Heart mean to you?

Isaac: (5 years old):
Expanding Your Heart means making my heart
as happy as the brightest sun.

INTRODUCTION

Have you ever been shaken to the core as the result of a life-changing experience? Was your life moving in one direction when suddenly something happened that altered your reality, and chaos ensued? Was your stability turned upside down, leaving you to question reality, and wondering whom to trust? Did you even question the meaning of your own life? The life-shattering experience may have come as the loss of a loved one to divorce or to death, a job loss, or losing your home; you may have experienced a health crisis, an accident, or been in a natural disaster.

Do you find yourself asking: Why did this happen to me? How did I get to this place? Is there a bigger reason for what's happened? Before circumstances forced change, were you thinking about making a change in direction in your life? Are your core beliefs being stretched? Are you questioning everything and everyone and trying to find an answer that will make a lot of pain, hurt, betrayal, devastation, and/or anger disappear?

I know too well this place of upheaval. For me, panic attacks gave way to pain, which eventually gave way to loneliness, anger, depression, and ultimately, I found myself in a very dark tunnel. This happened to me at a young age, but it can happen to anyone at any time. What

I discovered through my experience is that I could not count on logic to make sense of things, but there was a silver lining in the otherwise dark cloud, an upside to this type of life challenge. Life-altering experiences offer us an opportunity to open a very important doorway into a life we may not have thought possible. By going *through the heart* to understand our experiences, we will come to see that major life changes represent breakdowns of our human self so our true selves can break through.

What I have learned is that not only do these breakdowns present doorways through which we can move into a life of fulfillment, but they actually represent a breaking open of the heart—and there are four levels to healing from this type of experience. In this book, I will share with you what I am calling "The Four Stages of a Spiritual Opening." These Four Stages came to me in the form of a spiritual download through my Divine connection after I had prayed—for a long time!—for a way out of my own dark tunnel.

Knowing these Four Stages will change your life. You will learn how the Four Stages apply to you, and how you can turn tragedies into the most empowering experiences of your life. All the people, male and female, with whom I have shared these strategies have personally told me that directly relating the Four Stages to their lives provides a bigger picture perspective that has enabled them to let go of whatever previously held them back, making it possible to move on.

This book can help you let go and move on as well. It will support you in understanding all the *Why?* questions that come in the wake of circumstances such as loss (including divorce), crisis, or tragedy. This book will help you see that chaos is part of healing, and it will guide you through a process that will enable you to heal from the hurt and pain that follow heartbreak and chaos. It will transform your awareness to such an extent that what *feels* like a negative life struggle shifts for you into an opportunity to discover who you truly are, what your purpose is here on this earth, and how you can live an aligned life of fulfillment.

How can I be so certain that this book will help you in all these ways?

I've been a healer my whole life, only I didn't know it initially. After I had a nervous breakdown at age nineteen, I began to understand that my over-sensitivity was impacting my already overwhelmed and very agitated nervous system, resulting in anxiety and panic attacks. Essentially, I was imploding. At that time, I experienced a Divine intervention where I had an encounter with an angel. My heart cracked open, and every block that existed in me between my heart and the heart of the Divine dissolved in the wake of that encounter.

On its own, my mind could not have overcome the mental blocks that were causing me pain, nor could it have relieved the pressure resulting in panic attacks. Coming face to face with an angel, however, instantly healed my anxiety. What came next for me was a faith-driven mission to follow my heart's calling, which included several years of chaos. Chaos because I felt I was too young and too immature to take on what was being asked of me. I had never experienced my over-sensitivity as a gift, but it is precisely this gift that, as a healer, allows me to see, hear, feel, and sense intuitively. I realized that if I didn't learn how to use my gifts, they were going to haunt me.

So I stepped onto the path of exploring energy healing and intuition. I was twenty-two years old when I formally started to study healing work. I spent years learning, practicing, and doing the work, but I never wanted to be a healer. I didn't take it seriously. It wasn't until I accepted that I was being challenged by life to look at the gifts I was given—and turn *to* them, rather than running away from them—that my life dramatically changed. After I accepted the truth of where my path was taking me, my phone was constantly ringing with calls from people asking for healing sessions. By the time I was thirty, I had over 300 private clients, whom I'd see in-person or connected with by phone. My healing practice was sustained entirely by word of mouth. I did no advertising. By the time I was thirty-five, I'd worked with over 500 clients.

Since then, I've published my own book, *Energy Healing Through the Chakras: A Guide to Self Healing* (2009), and joined the likes of Wayne Dyer, Brian Tracy, and others as a contributing author to *Bouncing Back: Thriving in Changing Times* (2008). I've conducted courses in developing intuition, both online and in-person. In 2011, I began my Healer Training Program, where I train others in my Held in Light healing method. This groundbreaking program was eventually offered concurrently in four different cities in the U.S., and it continues today as an online course with participants from all over the world. I have been interviewed about energy healing for television, magazines, and radio, including four times in 2013 and 2014 on WFSB/CBS TV's feature *Better Connecticut*.

Now that you know a little about me, let's go back to the question I asked above, which you may still be asking yourself: How can I be so certain that this book will help you step out of your pain and into your truth and light? I am certain because, from its beginning until today, my work has consistently followed my original calling: to help people like you step into the light of who you are, clear your mental and emotional blocks, and live a more Divinely connected life. As my own awareness expands, my skills as a healer deepen and evolve, but in everything I do, I remain true to my heart's calling as a healer. This book is just another expression of my gifts serving my mission.

I understand that a spiritual approach might not feel like an appropriate fit for some people. "Energy healing," you may think, "is not my cup of tea." It's understandable, too, that you may have been living with your wounds for so long now that it might be scary to open up and examine them. I can tell you, though, that for the vast majority of people I've worked with, feeling the fear about what they will unearth is far worse than anything that actually comes up for them. When you have the support of a tested model for healing (based in Divine love), together with an understanding of how energy is stored in your body, and why your soul is called to experience major transformation, your life can improve for the better.

Life is a series of experiences, and there is a lot of shadow in this world. Shadow is unprocessed pain and emotions. When pain is not dealt with, it lies dormant in the energetic body. Many people behave irrationally based on this pain, rather than dealing with and moving past the pain.

We are not meant, however, to live in the shadow, or to live from our wounds. Our mission in life is to find the light within us and to live from that glow. Living from our inner light is living in truth, and each light has enough power to change this world. Healing your wounds makes it possible for you to turn any tragedy into an empowering contribution to life. Fear, disconnection, pain, doubt, and lack of faith are what hold you back because your heart is always going to guide you to life experiences that bring you joy, love, peace, acceptance, and fulfillment. To keep fear and other negative feelings from blocking us, we need to experience a spiritual expansion from the heart. This book's purpose is to help you experience that expansion.

As you read, I will be your guide on your journey to open your heart and begin your spiritual expansion. Everyone of us has what it takes to move through this process: If I can do it, so can you. What's amazing is that once begun, spiritual expansion continues throughout our life-time, and free will is how we deepen that expansion in our lives. I'll share more of my story with you in this book, and you will also read stories of others who have gone through spiritual openings. You will hear what chaos and healing looked like for them. I would venture that you may have your own story of a spiritual opening, and you may even have been seeking a way out, looking for reassurance that there is a way to move through the aftermath and heal. I am offering you a way to reframe a breakdown or tragedy from a spiritual perspective, and to guide you through the healing available that will allow you to experience the greatest expansion your heart has ever known.

This book is for you if you are standing at the gates of your own heart, ready to walk in—possibly afraid, cautious, hesitant, maybe even needing permission to know it's okay to begin. If you are now beginning, or have already been on your heart's journey for a while, this book will provide context and a relatable story about how you can turn pain into empowerment. You will most likely be challenged, and it may even hurt, but it will be worth it. In these pages, you will learn to reframe traumatic life experiences as you gain understanding of how the Four Stages of a Spiritual Opening are actually occurrences of the Divine at work within you.

Are you ready to begin? Are you ready to heal your life? Are you ready to put the story of being stuck and broken, being hurt and in pain behind you? Are you ready to find your true Self again? If so, let's step out on the path together.

With love,

Wendy Darost

AN INTRODUCTION TO THE FOUR
STAGES OF SPIRITUAL OPENING

In 2008, I was on a hike reflecting back on my life journey and how I actually came to be an intuitive. While hiking, I often pray and connect to the Divine, transforming hiking into a form of walking meditation for me. On this particular hike, I received what I refer to as a profound spiritual *download* concerning the stages of my spiritual opening and how it would finally become possible for me to accept my calling.

The information I received showed that there are Four Stages of a Spiritual Opening. Many people experience these Four Stages regularly, but lacking awareness of how these stages present themselves and the meaning they bring, it becomes easy not only to think the universe is conspiring against us, but also for it to feel natural to consider ourselves victims of circumstance. Through the lens of awareness, however, the Four Stages actually provide an empowering approach to what might seem like a victimizing situation: In the guise of a life challenge, the Soul is directing change so that the body, mind, and spirit can come into true alignment with the Divine Heart.

After receiving this download, I began reflecting on my own life and how true this felt for me. Cherishing what I'd received on this eventful hike, I rushed home to write down the information I'd taken in about the Four Stages of a Spiritual Opening. Eventually sharing this new perspective with others, I heard from friends and clients alike that these Four Stages made perfect sense and gave them a map for understanding some difficulties they had endured. My prayer is that these Four Stages help you feel empowered through your own personal evolution.

The Four Stages of a Spiritual Opening include:

The Initial Heart Opening

While an Initial Heart Opening can feel like a breakdown, it is actually a revelation. Truth is revealed, blindfolds are removed, and we come to see how we have been living something other than our truth. What happens to trigger this opening can be a health crisis, a relationship breakup, or the loss of a home or loved one. An Initial Heart Opening can feel like the rug is being pulled out from under us. While Heart Openings can often be traumatic experiences, they can also come about as a result of joyous occurrences, such as a marriage, the birth of a child, or a major life upgrade. At the core of an Initial Heart Opening is your decision, at the soul-level, to make a change, which directs you to dismantle structures and delve into the unknown. It's important to remember that you are guided into these experiences by the innate intelligence of the Divine at large as well as the Divine within you. An Initial Heart Opening essentially cracks open consciousness, allowing you to achieve greater union with the Divine in your life. What you may have experienced as heartbreak becomes the greatest breaking open of your spiritual heart.

Chaos

Chaos is the stage that occurs in the wake of an Initial Heart Opening. Chaos is happening when structures that supported who you were before your Initial Heart Opening begin to fall away. Chaos might also be the inner state you were experiencing before the Initial Heart Opening took place. The state of Chaos feels un-grounded, foggy, and confusing as you shift away from old attachments. In Chaos, you move through the unknown, which can seem fearful. The gift of Chaos is the imperative necessary for you to develop a strong sense of self and listen to your intuition since you may not be able to rely on the external, previously reliable, sources for security. Chaos requires that you turn inward to build spiritual strength. The various cords you've extended out to others and to situations start to flap energetically, and it is your work to pull those cords in and ground them into yourself. Cords are energetic lines of energy that bond us to people, places, things, and situations. Cords help us feel secure until we build more inner security. Then, unnecessary cords dissolve. When you strengthen your sense of self and your intuition, it becomes possible to build a deeper level of trust between you and God. How can this happen when you are triggered, scared, not sure how to settle, overly emotional, and most likely confused? It happens through Healing, which is the Third Stage.

Healing

Chaos and Healing can actually take place at the same time. Yet healing is also what you chose to move out of Chaos. Healing is the stage where major transformation happens. During Healing, you take responsibility for everything that has brought you to where you are now. Rather than seeing yourself as a victim, you see yourself as someone who is evolving through your life experiences. It requires looking at old wounds and taking stock of how you were responsible for contributing to your own suffering. Within these revelations, you find the power of forgiveness, the power of truth, the power of moral standing, and unwavering faith. Healing necessitates a fearless connection to the Divine, strong faith, and commitment to living your light in the world. Healing requires you to feel your emotions, let go of the past, separate out the Ego from the Soul, and be willing to see your light.

Contemplative Being

The stage of Contemplative Being entails living with increased awareness after having gone through the first three stages, and it's living with an expanded heart consciousness. In Contemplative Being, you are equipped with more personal tools for handling emotions and life's challenges. There is more connection to your Self and to the Divine in daily life through your own personal practices and daily awareness. In the past, most nuns, monks, priests, yogis, and disciplined practitioners entered the monastic life in order to achieve this state of heightened awareness. In our day and age, however, the current shift in consciousness means that we are all being called to live as Contemplative Beings in our daily lives. In this state, we have an understanding of the separation between the Ego and the Soul, and we are practiced at going inward. By connecting with our souls, we recognize that we are more than our wounds (more than our *story*), and by raising consciousness within ourselves, we are contributing to the global unity of peace, love, and compassion.

Contemplative Being is a state of living Divinely connected. It does not mean we become saints. It means we live connected—

we take responsibility for our actions, reactions, emotions, and aspects of our shadow. In Contemplative Being, we have healed enough to experience a mindful balance between living from the light and witnessing the shadow at work in our lives. The heart field is expanded to include self-love, self-awareness, spiritual love, and love for humankind. Contemplative Being can coexist with the states of Healing and Chaos. This fourth stage entails living with a powerful placement of the Divine serving as an anchor, keeping us rooted no matter the obstacles that come our way. This stage grounds us into a full acceptance that' we are Divine Love. In Contemplative Being, we have a strong spiritual *practice* of mindfulness, connection to Source, meditation, and embodiment of spirituality.

When I have shared these Four Stages with participants in my workshops and trainings, many have responded that they have lived these Four Stages without understanding how they are connected or what they mean. One workshop participant shared the story of her terrible divorce, how she couldn't see straight for a number of years, and how her life was in chaos. Prior to the *terrible* divorce, she had not been living her full potential, but once the journey of self-healing took place, she was able to see the Divine at work, and she came to understand why her divorce was necessary. Reaching this point of understanding that one's spirit has not abandoned him or her but was fully onboard throughout the journey through challenging times is eye-opening and affords people a sense of relief. Participants also share with me the feelings of hopefulness and gratitude they experience when they can acknowledge that seemingly traumatic situations are not failures.

The Four Stages will bring you hope, understanding, peace, and revelation. As you read about the Four Stages in the following pages, perhaps you will immediately think back to times in your life that were difficult. Rather than referring to that time in your life as negative, you may actually begin to move fully and mentally, physically, and emotionally past that time period and into living your true self in the present moment by having the context of the Four Stages. In Part I, I share my story of moving through these stages. You may find you have a relatable story to mine. When you read further into the chapters on the Four Stages, keep a journal handy. It may help to jot down some insights, revelations, or memories that come to you. Writing down your thoughts can help clear your mind and process some old energy from your consciousness.

PART I

PREPARING FOR YOUR
HEART EXPANSION

Chapter 1

MY EXPANSION

*"A bird doesn't sing because it has an answer,
it sings because it has a song."*

— Maya Angelou

Until I was in my early twenties, I had no idea I had a gift for healing, or that the work of healing was what I would be doing with my life. I didn't seek it out; I was called to do this work, and I had to let go of some attachments that were very dear to me and quite painful to let go of so I could undertake that calling. I could not have predicted that my life would open up the way it did—and continues to do every time I affirm my mission by saying, "Yes, I accept!" That said, I absolutely went through the Four Stages, and I share my story so you can see how your life may have followed a similar pattern to bring you to this place of reading this book to prepare for the next step in your journey.

In the Beginning, I Dreamed of Music

As far back as I can remember, I wanted to be a rock star. I began playing music when I was five years old. At least that's when I had my first guitar lesson. On a shining spring day in 1980, my mom dropped my brother and me off at our local church for a group guitar class. I remember hearing music pouring out of the room where we were headed as I tagged along behind my brother, Dave, who was two years older than me. We entered the room, joining the thirty-odd people already there, every one of them with guitar in hand, strumming away, roughly in sync with a man who held up cards, each card bearing a big block letter. I would soon learn that the letters showed chord changes.

As I looked around and saw everyone strategically fingering the necks of their guitars, I froze from the fear and humiliation of being left out, with no idea what these flashing finger forms were all about. Tears came, at that age probably from a deep-seated tendency to over-achieve: I hated not knowing how to do something! As impossible as it seems now, I was not taking into consideration that everyone else in the room (aside from Dave) was anywhere from fifteen to fifty years older than me, and they all probably had at least a tad more time invested in playing the guitar than I had at that point.

There I was, tears in my eyes, overwhelmed with feeling unable to speak the language. I was the youngest person in the room, and the guitar was so big that I could hardly wrap my arms around it. I stuck out like a sore thumb. I tried to look at and copy what my neighbor's hands were doing, but they were moving too quickly.

Finally, like an angel coming to save me from my own fear of not knowing how to get this guitar thing right, a sweet woman came over to my brother and me. She took us into another room and taught us the chords the group was playing, but I still couldn't play them because my fingers were so small. That was my first guitar lesson. It also was my introduction to playing music—something that would heal me and hurt me in equal measure as I progressed through life.

Breaking Down

I am the second oldest child—but the oldest girl—in a family of eight children. My parents were Italian Catholics, and ours was a loud and boisterous household. As a young girl, I wasn't sure why my parents had eight kids, and every time I asked, my mom would say, "Well, which one would you want to send back?" Of course, I always had a candidate to offer her. I was the oldest girl to siblings being born every couple of years, which forced me to play a maternal role that most of my peers wouldn't encounter until, grown up, they had children of their own. I could write a whole book on growing up in the De Rosa household, but that would take this story in a completely different direction. Suffice to say, my caretaking/healer qualities were already developing in those early, formative years.

I was a very sensitive child, but also a determined one. I had this way of sweeping up the emotions in the room and taking care of things around me, only to retreat later in angst because I wasn't getting the nurturing, attention, or space I needed to feel well. I would find my own quiet space where I could go inward to think, imagine, and create, and it was here that songwriting kept me company. Music was my outlet for disengaging from an overly emotional family and for going inward to process my own feelings. After my shaky start with the guitar, the piano became my instrument of choice to defuse and release my feelings. Despite my caretaker role in the family, I was headstrong and something of a rebel, so I instinctively knew how to keep the family pain from holding me back. Between the ages of ten and seventeen, I would sit at the piano every afternoon, go inside myself, and let my music comfort me. I would write songs and play any piece of music that would speak to me. I remember this sense of escaping into another reality while playing music, and it was heavenly because the stress and overwhelming feelings in my life were more painful than I could manage at the time.

I spent the majority of my youth singing, performing, and acting, completely driven and absolutely certain that music was my path. In truth, this drive was fueled by a need to escape pain, because at the time, I was a very wounded, accommodating adolescent who could see beneath the surface, but I didn't dare trouble the waters enough to be received or truly understood. It was safer to stay sweet and respectful to the needs and feelings of others than it was to make my own voice heard.

Being the oldest girl in a large family, a lot of responsibility was put on me to help raise my siblings. I grew up quickly and learned to live for others at a young age. I knew how to change diapers by the age of seven. By twelve years old, I started to nanny for families in my neighborhood. By fourteen years old, I had twenty-one families I nannied for, and I would sub-contract jobs out to my younger sister. My stress primarily came from not being able to be a kid. Instead, I was raised in a household of erratic emotions, poor boundaries, and over-responsibility.[1]

I spent so many years swallowing my own feelings and taking on the feelings of others that I blew up like a balloon, physically and emotionally. I was chubby, despite being very active. Frustrated by this

---

1 Here, I'd like to add that, as an adult, I can see that my parents did the best they could with the circumstances presented to them. The challenges I faced have shaped me into the person I am today. My parents are very loving people, and the struggles we faced did not change that. My purpose for telling my story is to show how my process of spiritual growth unfolded for me.

anomaly, I could only explain it as emotional weight and protection. My sensitivity intensified until I could no longer tolerate traffic, noises, large groups of people, loud music, or violent movies. Although music had been my outlet, I wasn't playing much in the later years of high school.

In 1993, I moved away from Connecticut to go to college in Boston, but I couldn't take my piano with me. I sang in choirs, but I no longer had my main processing tool. I had bouts of anxiety from time to time, but I remained unaware of the mounting symptoms. Within two years, however, the feelings of being overwhelmed came to a head. The overly inflated balloon that was me burst, and I experienced my first heart opening. That's how I describe it now, but back then, it was a panic attack.

I cracked. One day, the room I was in began to spin, and I hyperventilated. This earned me a trip to the school psychiatrist, who immediately put me on Prozac. Confused and emotional, I complied and took it for two weeks. Days into it, I'd regained my wits enough to be concerned that I'd been put on this medication without having been asked what was going on for me. I did not need medication; I needed someone to talk to. I needed a safe place to dump everything that had been dumped on me. I needed to have a good hard cry, and I needed to be heard. At nineteen, I'd thought that breakdowns only happened to people in their fifties after they'd lost everything in the stock market; this couldn't be happening to me. I took myself off Prozac and woke up to the probability of needing to leave school.

The most difficult years in the life of my family happened while I was away at college. Hearing bad news from my siblings and parents contributed in part to my breakdown. My instinct told me there was a way out of this, so I just had to find it in myself to take steps in a different direction. One of my college friends from Boulder, Colorado, felt un-settled in Boston and always spoke so highly of Boulder. Every time I saw her, it was like seeing crisp clear mountain air and a big blue sky. To me, she represented an amazing sense of embodied, home-on-the-range freedom and boundless hope. "I want that!" I thought because I couldn't tolerate the city life. My entire being was drawn to Colorado, so I decided to move there. This decision made no reasonable sense whatsoever; it was a pure calling.

Then the Angel Came

One night, after my recovery, my college roommate and I decided to go for a walk down Newbury Street in Boston. Despite it being a chilly night, it felt good to walk after all I'd been through. The question I was trying to work out in my mind was: Should I finish out the semester at school, or should I leave right away, in my post panic-attack state? Having just gone through an emotional breakdown, it was a stressful decision for me to have to make; I couldn't find my way clear to making a rational decision.

As I puzzled over my situation in my mind, struggling to find an answer that would bring me peace, my friend and I were approached by a man carrying a ukulele. He asked whether he could sing us a song in return for spare change. We brushed him off, saying, "No, but thanks anyway." Then the man looked at me and kindly stated, "I think you need to hear a song. Don't worry about the change." From that moment, I was mesmerized by his presence. He was dressed simply, wearing a red jacket. He had sandy-colored hair, and his head glowed as if surrounded by a halo. All at once, the whole world around me faded away; the street disappeared, and all I could see was this person with an angelic glow around his head. He told us his name was Arias, and then he began his song: "Home on the range where the buffalo roam…one day you'll get to Colorado...." I was in shock hearing his lyrics because it was as if he knew what my struggle was. Then he said to me: "Wendy (he addressed me by name), it's not time to go yet; you will get there; just hang in there a little longer," after which he kissed me on the cheek and ran off behind us. My roommate and I both looked at each other for a split second in disbelief, and then we looked back to see where he had gone, but he was nowhere to be seen. We walked up and down the street and looked in the shops, but he had completely vanished.

We were filled with the most astounding elated joy because we realized we had just experienced an angel. There was no doubt in our minds about it. I called my mom, who was a prayerful woman, and probably the only one who'd believe my story at the time. She said: "Wendy, I prayed and sent that angel to you. Your guardian angel's name is Arias."

Whether I'd met an angel or not, a miracle had occurred that night because following my encounter with Arias, the emotional suffering I'd been experiencing went away. I had received a healing. I finished out the semester at school aided by a renewed energy and the inspiration of Divine support. And from that point on, I felt I was being watched over.

My Initial Heart Opening

Following three semesters at college, I moved back to my parents' house in Connecticut to get my bearings and make a plan. After a few months there, I realized that my family home would not provide the supportive environment I needed at the time. Come summer, I went to Block Island, Rhode Island, where I was a nanny for dear friends and I also painted boats in the marina. It was a good resting place for me in the middle of the major transition I was experiencing. I was taking a period of time to recover from a major breakdown—what I now recognize was an Initial Heart Opening. My soul was making itself known to me through my heart, but I had no idea what should come next.

I wasn't entirely through the heart opening, either; it would unfold further in Colorado. I had anticipatory fears of the unknown (moving to Colorado) that coexisted with the deep calling I felt about needing to be there. My time of rest on Block Island was purposeful, and it was there that I first started practicing yoga, which proved to be a saving grace for me. I also turned to an old resource for healing: music. Using what I knew from reading music and playing piano, I taught myself to play the guitar, and I began to play music again.

Never losing sight of Colorado, I used my time on Block Island to work, save money, recover emotionally, be with friends, and strategize. The strategy that enabled me finally to make the move came in the form of a boyfriend I met on Block Island, who lived in Colorado in the winters and on Block Island in the summers. Scaring my parents half to death, I told them I'd be moving to Colorado with this new boyfriend in the fall.

Colorado: Moving in the Direction of My Heart

I started out for Colorado in September of 1995. I felt like a pioneer journeying west for the first time, trading in the traditional horse-drawn covered wagon for a 1987 Subaru wagon. I imagine, though, that the awe-inspiring view of the majestic Rocky Mountains moving closer on the horizon affected me and the pioneers in similar ways. The rising Rockies were a spectacular sight that left a strong imprint in my mind, a token of the conscious choice that I was moving on and up in the world. Twenty years old, undergoing what felt was like the purification of my soul, I was putting right all that I had been through as I journeyed across the grassy plains to make a new life for myself. I could feel in my bones, all the way to the marrow, the meaning of John Denver's lyrics in "Rocky Mountain High."

In retrospect, the significance of my nervous breakdown makes complete sense to me. I was a young girl with needs and feelings, but nothing in my life gave me permission to acknowledge my needs or feel my feelings. I had suppressed my own feelings in favor of taking on others' emotions until my heart could no longer take it. My heart had to break open so I could live *my* life, including accessing the gifts I wasn't even aware I had at that time. While I was experiencing extreme pain, however, I couldn't see how my breakdown was a good thing. It wasn't until much later that I saw the growth that came through feeling my feelings. Then I appreciated the strength that comes from experiencing a breakdown. After that breakdown, I never went back to taking on energy the way I had done before, unconsciously. My body just wouldn't do it because the programming to do so simply wasn't there anymore.

Leaving my family on the East Coast, I relocated to the West with a very clear inner agreement that I would never go back to living a life that included the suppression of my own life force so I could take care of everyone and everything else around me. The nervous breakdown I experienced was a breaking open of my heart—the first I'd experienced—and years later, I could clearly see that, painful as it was, it served as a catalyst for harnessing my life force for the benefit of my own life. That said, I still wasn't sure what all this meant, practically. At this point in my life, it felt as though what I would come to call Chaos and Healing were happening simultaneously, and this stage lasted for a very long time.

I headed to Steamboat Springs, Colorado, where I spent a year settling in and getting used to my new home. I decompressed in the mountains, worked at a coffee shop, and hung out with new friends because, somehow, I seemed to have more time for that now. Time and space appeared to work differently in the mountains. I experienced a second heartbreak when the relationship with the man who'd brought me out West came to an end. I didn't quit the mountains, though. Instead, I hiked and let myself be nurtured by nature and the amazing female friends I had around me.

When the Student Is Ready, the Teacher Will Appear

Wanting to find my way back to college, I moved to Boulder, Colorado, in the fall of 1997 and began classes at the University of Colorado. My re-entry into college proved confusing and chaotic for two reasons. First, I had difficulty finding my way. Second, I felt an initial blossoming of my intuitive gifts, but lacking an appropriate context for them, I was so empathic that I struggled with being in crowds of people. I also struggled in academia because my brain didn't process information the way it was taught. I would get confused, flustered, and emotional over assignments. It felt like my brain couldn't compute the information. I was very friendly, but I would withdraw when people tried to get close to me. Looking back, I was probably socially awkward. I was pursuing a college education because that's what was expected of me. It wasn't the education I needed to develop the true gift within me. Today, I know that people learn in different ways and college was not the right path for me. I wanted it to be, but it wasn't. I even went back to try to finish, but my business was thriving so much that I was pulled back to what was true to my heart. I do not regret that I never finished because, as it turned out, bigger things awaited me that would lead me to my life purpose, and finding that has always been worth more to me than a college degree. It was only through an unfortunate situation that I ended up in a perfect opportunity for my gifts to be nurtured.

When I was twenty-three, a whiplash injury I sustained in a minor car accident landed me in a chiropractor's office. Part of my recovery plan involved getting massages, and the massage therapist who worked on me also happened to be an intuitive. "I think you should go see my mom," she told me one day. "She's an intuitive healer, and I think you have this intuitive ability and she can help you." So I did go see her mom, who eventually became my healing teacher.

A soft-spoken, youthful looking woman, my healing teacher was the mother of six grown children and a grandmother to four. She was a powerful intuitive and her humble presence radiated her embodied wisdom. Possessing a curious social shyness, she was gentle and sweet. Her long, dark hair framing her soft white face was reminiscent of a cross between Snow White and a wise sage. We met for a healing session, during which time she not only confirmed my gifts, but she informed me that she'd soon be starting a class where she could teach me about being an intuitive and guide me in the use of my gifts. With pure excitement, I jumped at the offer.

What I learned from her provided an empowering reframing of my character traits, tendencies, and coping strategies that had previously caused me suffering. I found out, for instance, that my over-sensitivity and propensity for absorbing energy as a child were indicators that I was an empath. I also learned skills and tools I could use to help others with my intuitive gifts, without being negatively impacted by their energy or ending up depleted. Five other students like me were in the class, and together we studied with our teacher for almost two years, during which time she provided the education, insight, healing model, and framework for the work I do now. I left that initial training feeling like I had an outline and some basic know-how for the work, but it remained for me to bring heart and soul to it so I could make it my own—an expression of my particular light. It would take me the next six years to step into my own as a healer. This did not mean I was done with heartbreak: I would still have to go through a number of life experiences that left me heartbroken before I could more fully come into my heart.

Training to be a healer did not mean I had given up my dream to be a musician. By this time, I was a twenty-three-year-old, guitar-playing singer/songwriter who played in coffee shops, at concert venues, and sometimes with other musicians. Music continued to be an important way for me to process my thoughts and feelings. I did so for the next five years while doing intuitive healings on the side. In 2002, I decided to move to the San Francisco Bay Area to see where music would take me, entirely unaware that this route would land me in the center of an intense struggle and eventual heartbreak around music. I could not have foreseen what hardship I would have to endure before I could eventually accomplish what I was put on this planet to do.

Some musicians feel that if they are forced to stop playing music, they will die. That's not an exaggeration—that's how it feels, and that's how it felt for me. But in my case, it was my own heart telling me to let music go because there was somewhere else I was needed more. Imagine that: Your own heart telling you to let your dream die, to make room for something better! At the time, I had difficulty listening to my heart on this topic because I had worked my butt off, playing, touring, booking, promoting, all the while feeling an eager excitement that was completely ego-driven. At the time, I would never have admitted it, but in hindsight, I knew I was not pursuing a career in music from my heart: I was trying to prove myself worthy. As is often the case when we deny the heart, things don't always go our way, and true to form, I began to have one disappointing and chaotic experience after another when playing shows, which was tearing me up.

Two incidents in particular led up to one of the most important letting go experiences of my life. The first involved my guitar being stolen out of my car. All of my charts of songs, my journal of unfinished songs, and my cords/cables were also taken. For years after that, I choked up whenever I told this story because it was so traumatic for me. The act of losing everything in one fell swoop was not only devastating, but I couldn't make sense of it; I couldn't wrap my mind around its symbolic meaning. Even when I tried to take the high road, thinking I still had my health and I hadn't died, etc., it still felt like my heart had been ripped out of my chest, and consequently, I lost my voice. Literally, I lost my voice. For three years, I struggled with sore throats, hoarseness, and occasional laryngitis.

At this point in my life, I was actually doing healing work full-time, and I felt fulfilled and very happy with my work, but I still wasn't willing to give up music. I experienced a lot of joy from helping people through energy healing, yet I was doing the equivalent of sticking needles in my own eyeballs (i.e., making myself blind) trying to pursue music.

Waking Up, and Coming Home—to Myself

Shortly after my guitar was stolen, I travelled to a music convention in Austin, Texas, where I found myself walking with a friend down 6th Street on a Saturday night, around midnight. Wait…let me tell you what was really going on: I was in a parade of drunk people, all of us compressed into a two-block stretch of lit-up clubs that were spilling loud music and the stench of bar rot onto the street. Feeling like I was playing bumper cars trying to get from one end of the sea of drunk people to the other, I kept asking myself, "What am I doing here?"

Then it happened—the truth hit me! A couple who were holding hands walked toward me. I went to move around them so we wouldn't collide. At the same moment I moved out of the way, the man took his wife's hand, saying, "Honey, come here; I want to show you something...." As he grabbed her hand to pull her toward him, his hand collided with my nose! He had punched me right in the face!

Of course, the couple felt terrible, were overly attentive, and apologized profusely to me, while I, still feeling the impact of the punch, looked up and said to God, all the angels, the cherubim and seraphim, past ancient ancestors, and whomever else was up there laughing at me, "I GET IT. I get it. I get it. I get it." The sign was clear: I got the message. I had to get punched in the face to get it, but I got it.

I left Austin.

I quit music.

I stopped the Chaos.

I returned to the Bay Area and dove full force into my healing work. I put away my dreams of making it big with my music. I put it all away, and I listened to the voice I'd been ignoring, answering fully the calling coming from my heart. My healing practice really began to take off. I was expanding and growing as I was helping others to do the same. I never looked back, nor harbored any regrets about saying, "Yes" to what was in my heart. Years later, I let music back into my life, but this time, without an agenda and simply because I love to play.

I tell this story because what may seem like disparate threads did, in the end, come together to weave a tapestry that depicts the story of my heartbreak, chaos, and healing, all of which were instrumental in what became for me a significant and meaningful spiritual expansion. This was the beginning of my spiritual opening, but it was not the end; every day, my story of expansion continues.

You may have a relatable story that includes your own saving grace, helper, messages, and breakdowns that aided you in listening to your heart and truly expanding. On the other hand, maybe you have bits and pieces that don't add up for you, and it feels like you have experienced decades of chaos. Working through this book, you will learn how to hear and heed the voice of your own heart.

Chapter 2

THE QUEST FOR YOUR SOUL

"Ego says: Once everything falls into place,
I'll feel peace.
Spirit says: Find your peace,
and then everything will fall into place."

— Marianne Williamson

Understanding Spiritual Expansion

Once I fully embraced and honored my intuitive gifts through a commitment to healing work and yoga, my practice grew. Since 2003, I have had a full-time practice supporting clients who have confronted depression, emotional struggles, illness, loss, confusion, or trauma; they also consistently tackle questions related to living a more connected life. While observing the patterns inherent in my clients' physical and emotional struggles, I've noticed that much of their suffering stems from unrealized longings for deeper connection to Self and to the Divine. I see over and over just how much people want to open their hearts and how they want to feel in union with the heart of God—

only they don't always see from the outset that that is what they are actually seeking. Initially, they just want to feel better.

The telling questions that my clients bring to me include: What is my purpose? Where do I belong? How do I get through this? Why is this happening to me? These questions are a sure sign that a person is on a quest for his or her soul's intimate connection with the Divine. When starting to question one's purpose in life, the seeker is stepping onto his or her spiritual path. In order to answer questions about the soul's purpose, the seeker must quiet the mind and go deeper into the realm of the heart—because seeking questions serves as a gateway into the heart, which is where our true answers are to be found.

When I speak of the heart here, I don't mean the muscular organ in the middle of the human chest that pumps blood. I am referring to the spiritual dimension of the heart—the realm of the heart as a spiritual state of being. In order to meet the individual soul's need for fulfillment as a human being, the reasoning mind alone may not be sufficient. Feeling fulfilled is an experience of the soul; therefore, the mind will never be satisfied. It's through the heart that we understand contentment and the sense of being.

Ego vs. Spirit

It is important to understand that a spiritual quest is not an unmitigated joy ride. The spiritual journey of the heart will not necessarily be constantly blissful. But it will always be honest. The conflicting duality between the Spirit and the Ego is vital to spiritual expansion in human life.

The Ego is our small-s self-image; it is the personality we create in response to the external stimuli of life circumstances and experiences. Ego can manifest itself as being both healthy and wounded in our lives. A healthy Ego comes, essentially, from being held in esteem, either by others or by ourselves, and it enables us to express our true self in the world. The wounded Ego is the composite manifestation of our wounding in life—our defenses, programming, fears, and neuroses—that come into being as we seek to protect our vulnerable self from harm. The wounded ego supports unhealthy emotional attachments, whose goal is to create a sense of safety for the vulnerable self.

The Spirit, on the other hand, is our capital-s Self, our Soul, etc. It is the part of the Divine consciousness within us. Soul, Self, and Higher Self are all terms to describe this Divine consciousness in us. In this book, I will demonstrate that Spiritual nourishment and the healing of Ego wounds are required for the Soul's awakening and expansion to occur.

While writing this book, an array of intuitive images was revealed to me in my meditations. It was then I saw four distinct stages that people pass through while journeying on their spiritual paths; these stages result in the opening of the spiritual heart. These four stages might be easily mistaken as life-as-we-know-it, yet underlying them is the soul's integration with human life. They are a conduction center through which the mystical and the physical worlds meet, and they provide a supportive context for understanding how some challenging life experiences are not without purpose, but actually are in full Divine order. I will discuss this topic more thoroughly later as we delve into understanding the heart.

The Importance of Connection to Source

It's not hard to find people who, seeking meaning in life circumstances, ask why things happen the way they do. It is more difficult to find people who will commit to their own healing by engaging with the Divine, through faith, to find their own answers to the questions they ask. There are people who seek me out to help them solve life problems. When I ask them whether they have a personal spiritual practice that will support healing, they tend to reply either "No," "Not really," or "Occasionally." No matter my skill as a healer, I can only take people so far in the healing process. The greater part of healing is a highly personal, very intimate encounter between a person's soul and God. I can guide an individual to the meeting place, but then it is up to the person asking for healing to engage his faith and allow healing to happen. Healing and heart openings that lead to transformation require not only intimate faith between human will and Divine will, but first a level of surrender that allows for such faith.

Our Souls Are Born from Divine Light

No suffering exists in the light of the Divine, and the soul longs to dwell there; the soul wants to be light, to feel light, and it strives always to return to its natural state. While in human form, however, the soul is limited by the human condition, which includes the challenging aspects of an overactive mind, conflicting emotions, false notions of security, and material and emotional attachments. While it can be easy to live in denial of emotions, or disassociation from them, this merely compartmentalizes the Self from emotions, which is *not* at all the same thing as freedom from emotions or from suffering. Such displaced emotions can be felt by and impact others. Displaced emotions belong to the shadow—i.e., unconscious—part of our Ego. The work of healing involves realizing that the Ego is not our true Self. Our true Self is the individual spark of Divine Light within us.

We go through our normal, everyday human existence, not remembering our soul's memory of what freedom and joy in the Divine Light feel like. This disconnect, however, actually motivates us to remember who we are and rejoin the Source of our true Self. As long as we remain separate from the Light, we suffer. Though not obvious, perhaps, this separation underlies our human state of discontent, as we seek to find Divine joy in non-Divine, external sources. By connecting more deeply to the Divine through the heart, the joy and contentment your soul is seeking come readily into your life. The Ego will bring up the memory of wounds; the Soul, on the other hand, will bring to you the innate and deep love of the Divine Light within you.

The Role of Emotions in Spiritual Healing

In the same way that the planet contains shadow and light, so the heart has the capacity to hold contradictory emotions. If you've ever experienced tears of joy, you know what this feels like. You are so happy that tears come, coupled with grief and awe. Joy and sadness, for example, can exist at the same time. While the expression of dueling emotions confuses the mind, those emotions are easily held in the heart, which is not a rational place. To feel this duality is actually the sign of a wonderfully healthy, expansive heart. The thinking mind may want to isolate and focus only on positive feelings, but true spiritual growth happens when we are also courageous enough to feel the intense, perhaps heavy, feelings that dwell in the heart as well.

At first, intense feelings can bring a sensation of being overwhelmed. You may not even be able to identify the feeling itself apart from the overwhelming feelings—it may simply present itself as a swirling sensation. When you are in such a state, trying to think about what is happening is not at all helpful; you cannot rationalize feelings. Rather, connect to the sensations in your body, and breathe through them until your body has the ability to process the overwhelming state. This is *breathing into* a feeling or a sensation. In time, you may be able to separate out feelings from sensations, and you may be able to connect memories to emotions. The contrasting feelings arising in the heart may be connected with a loved one or relate to a situation. Reconciling and feeling the emotions of the past will allow you to decide consciously what you want to keep and what you want to release.

It is incredible how much we witnessed, internalized, and soaked up as children...*and* it is possible to breathe into the old emotions, release them, and actually move that energy in your body, making it available to you now, for the benefit of your current life.

While it can be challenging, visiting or revisiting the past and letting go of old emotions is incredibly freeing! Reconciling shame, embarrassment, anger, etc., and moving them out of your system makes it possible to create space for the expansion of self-love, peace, and contentment with life's current situations. What I'm describing here is the essence of a healed life: living in the present, without the baggage of the past, *rather than* living in the past, constantly trudging through old wounds and the suffering they create. Facing shadow emotions in order to make more room for love does require a great deal of courage. Not surprisingly, our word *courage* is derived from an Old French word, *corage*, meaning "heart, innermost feelings." It can feel vulnerable and scary to address the feelings in the heart. Yet knowledge is power. As you journey forward in this book, you will learn tools for spiritual and emotional healing. Once you know how to work with these emotions, feeling them won't feel so scary. Let's journey onward to understand a bit more about the heart.

Chapter 3

THE SACRED HEART

"The essence of any religion is good heart.
Sometimes I call love and compassion a universal religion. "
— Dalai Lama

Understanding the Heart

Before we explore the Four Stages of a Spiritual Opening, it's important to understand the complex nature of the heart, and in particular, the role it plays as a spiritual center. I've gained this knowledge from my long career working in the sacred space of the heart as a healer and as a yogi throughout the years. Although I did not elaborate earlier on how instrumental yoga has been in my life since I was eighteen, much of my awareness of the intuition and the energetic body came from my study of yoga.

The Three Facets of the Heart

The heart is composed of the following three facets:

- ♥ **The Physical Heart**: the physical muscle in the chest that pumps blood to all the organs in the body.

- ♥ **The Emotional Heart**: the *feeling* center of our being through which we experience empathy, compassion, grief, and anger. The emotional heart reminds us that we have human consciousness and the ability to feel for ourselves and others. The emotional heart desires human connection and positive feelings. It can be blocked from feeling, however, as a result of emotional wounding.

- ♥ **The Spiritual Heart**: the place where the Divine coalesces with human consciousness, by way of the Soul. Our Soul communicates innate Divine intelligence from our subconscious to our conscious mind.

This book primarily concerns the Spiritual Heart; however, each of these three aspects is extremely important for overall health. Although this book will not include in-depth information about the physical heart per se, as you read on, it's important to keep in mind that heart health is impacted by healing the emotions in the heart and by allowing for the spiritual heart's expansion.

The Universality of the Spiritual Heart

The image of the heart as the *seat of the soul* is not an original concept—it has been documented in a variety of spiritual teachings throughout time. While my experience of heart opening happened through my own meditations, and as a result of the life experiences I had, I also gained insights from other religions and spiritual practices. The two perspectives that spoke to me the most were Vedic and Catholic. My spiritual roots are in the Catholic tradition, but in my late teens, I rejected Catholicism and began to practice yoga. Now, I am rooted in, and passionate about, the experience of the Sacred, Divine energy and Grace, regardless of denomination. It does not matter to which spiritual practice or religion you belong because the experience of the Sacred Heart is open to everyone; it is not bound by religious affiliation.

The Vedic Perspective

The Vedas are the oldest existing texts in the world and the sacred scriptures of the Hindu religion. In the traditional teachings of yoga, the image of the Spiritual Heart is called the Hridaya, which is the center of Atman, the Higher Self. When Atman, or the Higher Self, is centered in the heart, it is in union with Brahman, which is the prevailing, absolute consciousness (perhaps perceived as the Universe or the Divine). When the Higher Self is in alignment in the heart with Brahman, the result is Moksha, or liberation (which is the Soul's freedom, in union with Divine Light).

This may sound a bit complicated, but bear with me:

The Hridaya is also not free from suffering because it is also connected with our inner knowing (or perhaps our conscious or subconscious remembrance) of suffering. This philosophy teaches that our Karma (our choices or actions in life) and Samskara (our innate sufferings) are part of being human. *This concept is the same as the Christian idea of a soul seated in the center of the heart in union with the Divine.* When seated in the center of the heart, the Self is in freedom, which is the returning to Light that was discussed in Chapter 2. Additionally, the heart can hold sadness and joy at the same time, which are conflicting emotions. The Vedic interpretation of this contradiction is that the Hridaya (Spiritual Heart) is the source for both liberation and karmic suffering. Through spiritual practice, we can learn how to bring freedom and peace from human suffering.

My point is that in many religious traditions, the spiritual heart offers an experience of overcoming human suffering (emotions) in order to feel free.

Yoga is Unification of the Heart

The way to achieve this inner peace offered by the spiritual heart is through deep meditation and the quieting of the thinking mind. Yoga is one method that aids in this goal; it is more than just doing poses and relaxing the body. *Yoga* is a Sanskrit word that means *to join* or *to unite*. One definition for the discipline of yoga is: *the joining of the fragmented parts of our being, coming into unity in the heart, the dwelling place of the soul.* The twenty-first century translation of this idea sounds a little less poetic, but it is no less profound: healing the pain of past experiences. If you have a wound that remains unhealed, part of your soul has not left that experience, which leads to fragmentation. As you walk around in the present moment, part of your soul is still living in the past experience of the unhealed wound. Learning how to breathe into the emotions related to the wound, forgive those involved (including yourself), and let go of that wound will heal the suffering you carry around that wound. (Please note: When the wounding goes very deep, or it is substantial enough in size that you are not able to work through it on your own, not only is patience required, but you will probably need additional support from therapists, body and/or energy workers, etc.)

Patanjali's *Yoga Sutras* affirm the importance of quieting the mind and establishing discipline and awareness for the purpose of living a life in *union* with your soul and with the Divine. The way to realize this union is through truthful living and daily practice. Yoga asana (or poses) are designed to clear the meridian system of our energetic body where energy blockage can exist. When the body is clear, the mind can settle. By clearing blocks in our energetic body, aligning the physical structure, and quieting our thoughts, we create more space for the soul to drop into the heart.

Energetic Anatomy and the Heart Chakra

Within Vedic teachings, the "anatomy" of the subtle, or energy, body is comprised of a network of energetic meridian lines (nadis), pressure points (marma), and power centers (wheels of energy called chakras). The chakras have now made their way into the Western awareness and are commonly known to many Westerners as a familiar facet of metaphysical healing. If this is the case for you, you may have figured out that the Heart, to which I refer in this book, corresponds, of course, to the Heart Chakra. The Heart Chakra is the melting pot of spiritual love and human love. We connect to our soul through the Heart Chakra. Similar to the Heart Chakra, the Hridaya, or Spiritual Heart, is the center of life force and spiritual dwelling for the soul. The Hridaya, however, is also the source of connection to the prevailing, absolute consciousness of Brahman, which makes it possible for us to live in union with all things. In other words, when the Higher Self has quieted the thinking mind to such an extent that the Soul can *be* in the heart, there is a deep knowingness and feeling state of unconditional love and connection to all of life. This is the state of being in unity, at one with all creation.

The Sacred Heart

I find it so interesting that we have so much conflict between religions because, at heart, the core teachings of many spiritual practices and religions are saying the same thing. The Christian equivalent of what I have just described from the Vedic perspective is the concept of the Sacred Heart. This was something I'd learned about in my Catholic upbringing, which vividly returned to me years later in my study of spiritual openings. I became aware of the Sacred Heart as a symbol of Jesus' prevailing love for humanity, which ultimately led to his crucifixion. Similar to the Vedic Atman in union with Brahman in the heart, when the Sacred Heart of Jesus is filled with the light of God, the result is universal love for all beings. Images of the Sacred Heart depict a red heart with a crown of thorns, a cross, and a burning flame, symbolizing the crucifixion, human suffering, and the internal light of love prevailing. In the Sacred Heart, there is glowing golden light radiating from the heart, reminiscent of the image of the Heart Chakra radiating light throughout the whole body. The unconditional love depicted in these images includes the biblical story of Christ's crucifixion—again, a conflicting experience in heart. The story of Christ on the cross tells us: there was suffering, and there was liberation from suffering.

The symbol of the Sacred Heart was once manifested to one of my clients because she was being called to spiritual love at that level. The Sacred Heart had previously come into her awareness through her meditations without her having heeded its call. When it was brought to her attention again during a session with me, she decided to pay attention to it. I have not been a practicing Catholic since childhood, and this image had never shown up for me before. Sitting with this particular client, though, the strong presence of the Sacred Heart brought its meaning home to both of us. While she was sensing the strong call of this sacred symbol, she struggled to understand its relevance for her life. The Sacred Heart has always been a metaphor for Divine love dispensing kindness, healing, and compassion for human suffering. When my client realized she'd been living the experience of *carrying her own cross*, she laid down her unnecessary burdens and began listening to her inner calling, which she was finally ready to hear at this point. She actually only made a minor life shift after our session, which was to change jobs. The bigger shift happened internally when she felt filled with Grace after being touched by the image of the Sacred Heart.

For me, the Sacred Heart had encapsulated the image of spiritual openings that were initiated in the heart. The heart—the conduit between the Divine, the Soul, and all of life—was where we experience intuition and Divine calling.

As we learn to live life from the spiritual heart, we may have to pass through our own suffering, or crucifixions, because we cannot free ourselves from suffering by *avoiding* suffering. The prevailing love of the Sacred Heart, or the freedom of Moksha, necessitates an understanding that there are and always will be dualities (i.e., things that seem to conflict, such as suffering *and* freedom) in the realm of the heart as well as in life in general. Finding peace with this understanding will help you have compassion for your struggles, and it will set you on your way to hearing and heeding your soul's deeper requests and callings.

The symbolism of the crucifixion can appear in our own lives in a variety of ways. Sometimes, it means losing a home or a loved one, going bankrupt or to jail, falling ill, getting a divorce, or experiencing other types of major, unexpected changes. When this type of event occurs, it can feel like the world is caving in on you and God has personally chosen you as a target for punishment. But it is not personal at all. What's happening is the duality of life at play. While events such as these do tend to dredge up human emotion and engender struggle, they also present opportunities to overcome suffering, strengthen character, and bring about a more authentic state of connection with the Divine. We typically turn to faith—or turn away from faith—when we are facing challenges, or when we can't otherwise make sense of the world. When we choose to turn to faith, we find compassion for our own suffering. Living from faith, we come to understand that suffering is purposeful. If, rather than looking at life squarely, and taking on what we are facing, we turn away from faith at a moment of crisis, it is not uncommon that we will soon again be presented with "teachable moments," perhaps even repeatedly, until we learn the lesson inherent in the situation.

In the coming chapters, I will explain in detail the Four Stages and how to care for yourself as you maneuver through each one. As you read this book, you may actually discover that you are currently experiencing one of the stages described. My own story contains examples of three of the four stages of growth that occur when the heart experiences an opening. The fourth stage is continuous and ongoing for me as I stay open to my Divine Connection. Individually, these stages can last anywhere from a few months to a number of years; alternately, an individual might pass through all four stages within a few years. And the first three stages may repeat themselves many times before the fourth stage ever happens. Therefore, you may be experiencing one or more of these experiences at this time. I have provided numerous exercises and meditations to support you in moving through challenges that may arise during these four stages. It is always my intention to provide resources for healing and coming more into alignment within yourself and with the Divine.

PART II

THE FOUR STAGES
OF SPIRITUAL OPENING

Chapter 4

THE INITIAL HEART OPENING

"To open deeply, as genuine spiritual life requires, we need tremen-dous courage and strength...a kind of warrior spirit. And the place for this warrior strength is in the heart."

— Jack Kornfield

When we hear *heart opening*, we might think this term refers to a *reopening* of the heart after a period of having had the heart closed to love. We might even think of it as a door opening to allow us to feel free inside or feel our emotions more fully. While those are varieties of heart openings, this book is concerned with the *spiritual* aspect of a heart opening—when the Divine soul begins to commune with the physical body, leading to an awakened moment of consciousness, which brings about a shift in our perspective on life.

It is an awakened moment when the conscious mind aligns with the heart. When this happens, a person may quest for deeper knowledge, a heart-based experience of life, and a connection to God. This opening is often described as *a moment of clarity, seeing the truth, knowing your calling*, or an *aha! moment.* Conversely, a heart opening might entail a breakdown of some sort, a tragedy, or a wake-up call, which is then followed by a moment of truth. Once an initial heart opening occurs, it is usually followed by major life changes, including such things as a career change, a geographic move, a spiritual pursuit, making a pilgrimage of some kind—even ending an unhealthy relationship or changing a living situation.

Carmen, a social worker in California, who became one of my clients, shares her story of her initial heart opening below:

Carmen's Story

A few years ago, I had the biggest heart-opening experience in my life thus far. It happened through a breakup with my then-boyfriend. It was one of those breakups, as many people have, that allows you to get to the place of rock bottom. I'm sure many people can relate to this rock bottom place! For me, it felt like I was nailed to the Earth—that pain was grounding me securely to the present moment. Not only was I grieving the loss of this very important person, but the breakup revealed old wounds that the relationship had masked, and it challenged my sense of identity and life purpose. I was literally broken and breaking wide open. It would eventually lead to such enormous relief, such a wide heart-opening, but at the time, it was all I could do just to get by each day.

We dated for just a year. He was severely depressed, struggled with alcohol abuse, yet had a wide and beautiful heart. And in this year, I was trying very hard. I drove to meet him in the city, I washed his laundry, I cleaned his bedroom, and I listened to him intently every night at his favorite bar as he shared the perils of work and life. We existed in this world, kind of clutching on to each other.

What I didn't realize at the time was that all this energy I was expending toward him was masking a kind of desperation within myself—like I was fighting against loneliness, fighting to prove my worthiness in the world, trying very hard to make sure I was needed and deserving of love. The proof was going to be whether he loved and stayed with me. However, this way of being, it wasn't just with him—this belief system was woven in my job as a social worker, it was apparent in my friendships, and it was the driving force in my family relationships—I had to prove it to the world, and I had to prove it to God. I was worthy because I knew how to give of myself completely. I was duty bound to serve others by fixing problems, and my worthiness was found in whether I was successful and whether others loved me.

The night we broke up, I drove home alone to my studio. I sat on my couch and bawled. And I told God that I was done. I was done living in this world in this way. I was literally finished going about the world with so much loneliness. I remember saying aloud, "God, I can't do this anymore. I'm so tired. I'm done being in the world like this. I want to go home." The grief felt immense because I believe it was the grief of thirty-three years of trying so hard to earn love.

My body was in some kind of shock for a couple of weeks. I couldn't sleep through the night, and somehow, I didn't need to. I couldn't eat very much. My system was in utter chaos. And this led me to reach out for an energy healing from Wendy De Rosa. It was during this time that I heard direction that would forever change my life. I heard that my soul was starved for nurturance. That this relationship hadn't been all bad, but while in it, I had forgotten to replenish my heart with things that nourished my soul. I was told to find a church, to find tonal and vibrational healing, and to reach out for help. And so I did. I began listening, really listening to my desires. I started bearing witness to my heart.

I began going to a spiritual center twice a week. I was very real with my friends, and I let them know just how broken I was—I let them help me. I woke up every morning and wrote three pages to God. I downloaded spiritual books from the library onto my computer and rode to work playing them in the car. I sat taller at work to allow grace to flow through me, and I saturated myself with positive healing. If I felt like soaking in a hot tub on a Wednesday night, I found a soak. If I felt like eating chocolate ice cream for dinner on Tuesday, I ate ice cream. I listened intently to my own intuition in a way I never had before. I turned all of my attention fully toward my heart. And I gave it—really gave it—my love. It was in this awakening that my heart began growing stronger. It was in this way I found a relationship with the Divine I had never known possible. And I started feeling really light and joyful. There were signs everywhere that I was on the right path. That I was loved.

Without realizing it, I had a very strong, but unconscious, belief that having an expanding heart was all about over-giving of myself. I thought it was found through proof of how much others needed me. Some would call this codependent love. I call it painfully proving my worth. It was through reaching this dark and lonely place in the breakup that I had the chance to get in touch with how I was putting myself in a painful life position. It was painful not attuning to my own heart. And through this process, I found so much joy! I found that receiving love meant just tuning into prayer, tuning in to all the love around and within me at any moment. It meant being truthful toward my heart. Through expanding my own love, through tapping into Divine love around and within me, I started feeling energized. There was no going back. I found God within my heart. Divine Love was never outside of me. All this time, I had never needed to prove my worthiness. All this time, I was so completely loved within my own heart. I had love now to give, not out of proof to myself of my worth, but because my own heart, now more attuned, was more connected to its source, and full and loving. It was nourished and expanding. I had found home.

Carmen demonstrates here that by deepening her relationship with herself, she found love and nurturing at a deeper level. A need she had previously sought to meet through partnership was ultimately—truly—met through the journey she took into her own heart. From that place of fulfillment, she could hear her own heart's true voice.

To understand the Initial Heart Opening, it's important to know that our Soul has a higher wisdom or intuition, which sometimes contradicts what comes from the rational mind. We may understand this to be our conscious mind, made up of behaviors and beliefs of which we *are* aware, versus our subconscious mind, which is part of our being of which we are *not* aware, though we also operate from it. I will talk more about intuition later, but it's important to know how programmed thoughts work in the subconscious mind.

The Subconscious—Wounded Ego vs. Soul

The subconscious mind is not necessarily located in the brain. It is actually the intelligence that is carried in our energy field, and it transmits information to our cells. Dr. Candace Pert, a significant contributor to the emergence of Mind-Body Medicine as an area of legitimate scientific research, determined that cells have intelligence, and because cells make up the body, the mind is not in the brain alone; rather, the mind is in the body. What this means is that certain responses, actions, or beliefs may be programmed into the cells of our body as a result of past experiences, and at times, these responses, reactions, or beliefs may generate action that is contrary to what we intend with our conscious mind.

The Origins of Unconscious Programming

To understand better how the subconscious affects us, let's look at an example. Say a little girl in school eagerly raises her hand when the teacher asks a question because she thinks she knows the answer. However, her answer proves to be incorrect. The other children in the class laugh at her, and in that moment, time stops for this child. She freezes. She's humiliated. She has a physical response in her body where her skin gets flush, her muscles tighten, and she feels like she wants to crawl under a rock and die. At this moment, a physical imprint is being taken and the child records for future reference the following programming: "Be careful about speaking up because you might be humiliated." Even worse, she may never raise her hand again to answer a question from fear of being laughed at, shamed, or humiliated. While such subconscious programming is not beneficial for this little girl or any of us, this is a classic example of how information is imprinted in the body. From such an experience, the subconscious mind acquires the information it needs about humiliation to create tactics and strategies aimed at staying well clear of it. Even if, in the future, the little girl wants to answer questions and is positive she has the correct answers, she will not answer them until she overcomes this subconscious fear of humiliation. This example, therefore, clarifies how we often act in contradiction to our conscious intentions.

Based on such experiences, the subconscious mind broadcasts warnings over and over to the conscious mind, feeding back to us the doubts and fears we collect during hurtful incidents. In the end, how we think about ourselves is a product of these experiences as stored in our subconscious. When the subconscious part of our being has recorded a significant amount of information that is negative and contrary to the truth we preserve about ourselves in our heart and soul, what results are blindfolds to the truth, mental chatter, and a life lived in doubt and fear.

Ego

The two facets of our subconscious are the Ego and the Higher Self (or Soul). It is important to know the difference between these two facets and their individual roles in an Initial Heart Opening.

The Ego is the part of us that has an emotional attachment to the physical world and keeps us bonded to our prior conditioning in order to promote survival. Childhood bonding that is loving, supportive, encouraging, and positive leads to the formation of a **Healthy Ego**. The Healthy Ego will manifest our *true* selves in the physical world because it is by means of the Healthy Ego that we take potential energy and actualize it into physical existence. Our soul wants to manifest our true self in the world, and our Healthy Ego encourages us to move forward in life!

The **Wounded Ego**, on the other hand, is often fear-based and perpetuates mental chatter that can be victimizing at times. Its operating system runs on the unhealed parts of our history, biology, and unexpressed emotions. The job of the Wounded Ego is to keep us connected to our early childhood bonding around love and support because that's how we guarantee belonging and survival. If there were abandonment around our early understanding of love, for example, the Wounded Ego would prevent us from trusting others because it fears experiencing abandonment again.

The other aspect of the subconscious is the **Self, Higher Self, Soul**, or **Spirit**. (I often use these terms interchangeably.) This part of us is Divinely connected, and it has knowledge of the greater good of human existence. The Higher Self/Soul is the active Divine intelligence within us that keeps us aligned with our Divine truth. One way to think of it is to use the analogy of a moral compass. For example, if you know someone who is struggling with something in her life and you give her a flower to cheer her up, without second-guessing your action, it exemplifies kindness and consideration. We might say that your moral compass points you in the right direction. Like the pure act of a child, such gestures show innate human kindness.

Now, let's say that you recognized your friend was suffering, and you became critical: "What's wrong with so and so now? Why can't he just get over it?" Such criticism belongs to the Wounded Ego that is re-broadcasting the programming it carries from past experiences around dealing with pain and suffering, or it is reacting in response to it simply not having the heart capacity to hold space for challenging emotions. It's possible that this type of programming, which causes you to be critical of your vulnerable friend, stems from a parent criticizing you when you were vulnerable. Whatever its origin, this programmed reaction to your emotions, or the emotions of others, comes from the Wounded Ego. It's the part of you that retains and records how you bond emotionally to life. If your bonding were unsupportive or critical, the Wounded Ego tends to be critical, heartless, defeating, and victimizing—and not only to others—you might be the recipient of its most harsh criticism, and boy, can it chatter!

It is important to understand the Wounded Ego's role because many of us believe what it says to us! As children, what we truly wanted didn't matter or wasn't even considered. Instead, we did what we were "supposed" to do—we ended up conforming to what was externally expected of us in life because, before we heal old wounds, the Wounded Ego's voice is louder than that of the Soul. One of the reasons Initial Heart Openings happen to us is to level the playing field between the Wounded Ego and the Soul.

Globally, we are experiencing a significant rise in consciousness at this time, and your soul is part of that evolution. As you evolve, you outgrow the need to live from external expectations and other ways of being that no longer serve you. It is for this reason that people may choose to switch careers in the course of their lives; it also explains the so-called mid-life crisis. As a spiritually and consciously evolving species, it is natural for us to outgrow the costumes, masks, and false identities we have previously used. In my opinion, it is so much easier to live a life based in the awareness of this dynamic than it is to fall victim to the evolutionary path.

The Gift of Emotions

Feeling our feelings is an aspect of the Divinely connected life, whereas suppressing emotions or reacting to them are expressions of the Wounded Ego. Feeling emotions is a vital component of the Initial Heart Opening, and understanding emotions, feeling them, and connecting to them is a *core* part of our evolutionary path. As we begin to distinguish our Wounded Ego from our Soul, we become increasingly aware that our true self is not the negative thoughts and emotions we carry. On the contrary, we come to know that negative thoughts and unexpressed emotions are constructs of the Wounded Ego. Having a healthy way of understanding and processing emotions is an incredibly powerful way to let our Soul come through.

If you have not previously learned healthy skills around feeling emotions—talking about them, expressing them, or having support for
them—this information is important for you because *negative and
suppressed emotions clog clarity of the true Self.* We evolve through
releasing, healing, and processing our old emotions in a healthy way.
Reacting (rather than feeling), yelling, or blaming are pseudo-expres-
sions of feelings; they are not healthy ways of moving through stuck
emotions. For the most part, they are variations on a theme of spewing
anger. *An Initial Heart Opening is one way that life presents opportunities for our emotions to surface.* Conscious awareness of emotions
is another way to tend to feelings so their release can take place in an
empowering way.

What does conscious awareness of emotions look like? It means *fear*
of feeling is not present. Instead, there is understanding that emotions
come up for everyone, and just because a feeling exists doesn't mean
we have to be ashamed of it. Being aware of your own emotions and
allowing yourself to have them allows your body to release them,
as opposed to holding against the feeling for fear of feeling it. That
would keep the emotion in place. I'll say more about how to release
emotions as you read on.
I mentioned that the Wounded Ego is a product of our social, environ-
mental, and familial upbringing. The Wounded Ego records beliefs
about us specifically, and about life in general, that it picks up from
our family, from society, from what we see in the media, and even
from what we've internalized by watching others' emotional behavior.
Basically, we learn how to feel based on how those around us deal
with their emotions. An example is hearing a father say to a small
boy, "Quit crying! Boys aren't supposed to cry." When the little boy
hears those words, that belief system gets recorded and programmed

in his subconscious mind. As a result, the boy grows up learning to shut down emotionally any time grief or sadness show up. Or the man who was that little boy suppresses his emotions and disconnects when a tragedy or loss occurs. He may even say to himself: "Don't cry! Be a man!" This Wounded Ego chatter stems from a programmed belief that it is not acceptable to show emotions because being a man means suppressing them. Since we are human beings and part of being human is having human emotions, the suppression of emotion creates suffering for this unfortunate man.

Disconnecting from or suppressing emotions over time will often lead us to the experience of an Initial Heart Opening. If we go through life allowing the Wounded Ego to be right, protective, and entitled, the deeper flow of Divine intelligence within us will inevitably create a situation to confront the hubris of the Wounded Ego. An Initial Heart Opening does exactly that: It strips away the masks, the ego, the pride, and the fear, opening a way for our truer Self to come through and shine.

Understanding the *value* of feeling feelings is a crucial part of being true to ourselves. How many times have you heard someone say, "I'm fine. I'm totally fine. There's nothing wrong," but you know the person is not fine? That person is not being real! She is protecting and suppressing a true feeling. Of course, a boundary may be appropriate in that moment for a person not to express her truth, but if this is a long-standing way of being, truth is not being expressed here. *Others are more trusting of us when we are real with our emotions!*

How to Deal with How You Feel

It's through naming and acknowledging our emotions that we actually learn to manage them, rather than letting ourselves be consumed by them. What does this look like? Let's break it down into a three-step process:

Step 1: We must recognize that the recorded programming of the Wounded Ego is separate from the truth of our Soul. For example, when we feel fear about something, it is useful to ask: "What is the fear about? Is it truly something I should be wary of? Or is part of my Wounded Ego keeping me from experiencing joy and connection?" Sometimes, our Wounded Ego keeps us from experiencing what we desire to experience! The reason the Wounded Ego may prevent us from experiencing Joy is because there may not have been bonding to true joy in our childhood, which makes it a foreign experience for us. Remember that the Wounded Ego is created from our human experiences. The Soul, on the other hand, will always drive us toward life experiences that put us in alignment with the Divine, including love, joy, and peace.

Step 2: Naming an emotion can be freeing. Just to say, "I'm angry right now," as opposed to pretending you are not, or driving off in a rage or yelling at someone, is a responsible way of owning that emotion. Reacting (often over-reacting) to an experience or incident is another way of saying: "I have no understanding how to be in this emotion, so I will do or say something destructive, irresponsible, or boundary-less. In fact, I'll make it the other person's problem." Now, we're all human, and rare is the person who hasn't reacted to an emotion, as opposed to feeling it, at some point in life. That said, being truthful and vulnerable enough to say, "I am angry, and I need to take space before communicating," is a powerful way of taking emotional responsibility.

Step 3: How do you process your emotions? Here are a few suggestions regarding feeling and clearing emotions:

♥ **Breathe into them**. Direct your breath to the area of the body where the emotion is stored and breathe into it. Scan your entire body: arms, legs, feet, etc.; go as deep as your cells. Direct your focus to the area of the body where you are feeling that feeling.

♥ **Visualizing.** Create a visual to work with around the emotion, such as fire, smoky clouds, etc. If you see fire, for instance, how would you put out the fire? Think about what visuals you would create to clear/transform that image and its corresponding emotion.

♥ **Talk to the fear.** Ask it questions: Where did you come from? Did you come from me or someone else? How old are you? Do I need you anymore? Are you ready to go? If so, take some deep breaths and let it release down a long pipeline, through your body to your feet and to the center of the earth. This pipeline is your grounding cord and a useful tool we will come back to later in the book.

These are a few suggestions about how to process emotions when they arise. There are many other techniques you can use, but the main point is that gaining skills related to understanding emotions will determine the extent to which emotions support or hinder your full, spiritual expansion.

I have created a YouTube video called "What to Do When You Get Triggered." If you need some extra support on how to self-manage when you are in the middle of a trigger, refer to this video for further support. Just google "Wendy De Rosa What to do when you get triggered" if you're interested in seeing this video.

Initial Heart Openings Bring Us into Truth

Being honest with what you are feeling—living in Truth—is a way to put right what feels out of keeping with your integrity. Do you experience conflict between your heart's desires and your lifestyle? What needs to change? Being honest about what you are feeling takes courage, but it is how you will make space for your heart to open, allowing the Divine to meet you there.

At some point in a person's life, the soul may speak very clearly to her that something in her life needs to change. Trish heard that inner voice and chose to follow her inner truth. Below, she tells of the pain she experienced when those around her did not agree with her choice.

Trish's Story

At twenty-nine, I had everything I had ever dreamed of: a truly drop-dead gorgeous husband, beautiful twin boys of fifteen months, and a newborn baby daughter. We were living in one of the most beautiful cities in the world, had a small, but very character-full home in a great area, were surrounded by a large circle of friends, had loving and supportive families on both sides, and my husband had an upwardly mobile career. We were, as my sister-in-law liked to say, "The Golden Couple." As I type this story, fifteen years later, my husband and I are living on the same road, but in different houses. We have been separated for nearly ten years, and it was my choice to leave.

So how do I explain what happened between then and now? How do I explain leaving an apparently happy marriage, ripping my children's lives apart, rocking our social world, and devastating our families (and the aftershocks that kept coming)? What gave me the courage to do what I believed was the right thing for me, despite tremendous opposition and strong advice from those around me to the contrary? Friends and family tried to intervene in the most unexpected, direct, and confrontational ways. Strenuous opposition came even from my grandmother who, at my father's funeral, told me that my father's cancer was a direct result of the stress I had put him under because of my decision to leave my husband.

This many years down the line, the reasons are beautifully clear to me, although at the time, they were more intuitively felt. Ever since I can remember, my personal growth and spiritual development have been the guiding lights in my life. And something inside me, that "still small voice" was (and is) not going to let anything stand in the way of my path toward embracing those values. During those early married years, my relationship with my husband was mostly good, although highly volatile. Gradually, our lives began to separate and our connection, instead of strengthening, weakened. I sought counseling, but my husband steadfastly refused to join me in couples' work, explicitly stating that personal growth was not one of his highest values; he was happy as he was. And spirituality was not only a complete waste of time for him, but something he actively derided. After five years in therapy, I had to concede that either I was going to have to change, or I was going to have to leave. So I chose to leave.

To this day, I do not regret my decision. I made this decision to save myself. Selfish? Absolutely. But we all were hurting deep down. This was the path toward growth and freedom. It took a huge amount of courage to fly in the face of my love for my children and my desire for them to have happily married parents. It has been stressful, traumatic, heart-wrenching, and deeply sad. But I remain steadfast in my conviction that it was the right thing to do.

Six years after I separated, I found a partner who (for me) embodies the essence of all I hold dear—he is willing to learn with me, to walk the spiritual path with me, and is equally devoted to growth and freedom. He supports what is the most important thing to me, and that is a gift for which I am filled to overflowing with gratitude.

As for my ex-husband, he has a lovely new girlfriend of three years now, who makes him very happy. She is accepting of him completely, which has allowed him to grow and do all the things he loves doing. Because I was so unhappy with the direction our marriage was taking—and voicing it—in many ways he had felt like his choice of lifestyle and values were "wrong" in my eyes because they were not spiritual or introspective enough. This was very undermining for him, and he often felt "less than" or not good enough in my eyes. Not a recipe for his happiness at all. His new girlfriend accepts him exactly as he is—who he is works beautifully for her, and he is far more confident in himself and involved and able to pursue all the activities he enjoys with her blessing. She enjoys them alongside him, and she does not demand emotionally more than he feels good giving.

I get along very well with her, and we had a big "family" lunch about a month ago for my daughter's birthday, all together, which we enjoyed enormously. It has really taught me the value of understanding there is no "right or wrong," just what is the right path for each person.

What have I learnt? So much, but probably the most important is: You cannot live your life for others because that's not a life. Find out what is most important to you, and follow that. Very few things in life are truly black and white—most are just many, infinitely varied shades of gray. And it's up to you to have the courage to choose the ones that will color your life.

I consider these kinds of "wake-up calls" as heart-opening experiences because something critical happens to reveal that, on a soul-level, we are responsible for the life we create. Further, it is the heart that houses the deep wisdom of the soul, including its desires and intentions for life. In the heart, we hear our inner voice, a manifestation of the Divine.

In addition to Trish, I worked with a woman who told me her intuition had been giving her signals that things were not going well in her marriage. She had lived with childhood wounds around neglect, which she projected onto her husband. What was true for her is that she needed to feel loved and connected, but she did not know how to ask for that, or make it happen in her life because she had not been taught how in her early years. She had learned that the way to show love is to push people away, which is the exact opposite of what her heart needed and longed for. When she recognized her part in this dynamic, she was able to begin to heal that under-nurtured and unloved part of her personality. When she finally changed her behavior, she reported a profound feeling of clarity, personal power, and open, clear communication with her husband. The result? It helped their intimacy and saved their marriage.

When we are living a life not in alignment with our Truth, our bodies have physical responses to life circumstances. The soul is seated at the center of the heart; therefore, we may experience tremors in the heart if there is wisdom that needs to be recognized. Physically, experiencing a heart-opening may feel like panic, anxiety, a heart attack, heartache, or illness. From an intuitive perspective, however, these physical symptoms are a deep signal that out-dated patterns of behavior cannot endure much longer: something needs to shift in our lives, and it requires deep introspection and soul-seeking to initiate that change.

If we understand these kinds of experiences as heart openings and the soul's requests to feel connected to truth and to the Divine, then we will have the opportunity not to be victims when these experiences occur.

With Breakdowns Come Breakthroughs

The most useful connection I have made relative to this work is to understand the undeniable link between breakdowns and the need for spiritual connection. More often than not, emotional breakdowns, mid-life crises, heart attacks, heartbreak, and anxiety all reflect a deep need for spiritual connection in your body and in your life. Notice that anxiety, heart attacks, and emotional breakdowns all take place in the chest area—the seat of the heart chakra; it is from this place that your soul is trying to get through to you. In other words, *critical breakdowns are spiritual crises*. A spiritual crisis occurs when the Self in the body can no longer bear the suffering of the human psyche, nor go on in allegiance to the Wounded Ego, but it chooses instead to dismantle our old programmed structures to make space for a deeper connection to spirituality and consciousness so we may truly know God.

I find that those who do experience breakdowns like these (I will refer to these physical crises as breakdowns) are actually having *strength-building moments* because, in the end, they learn more meaningful ways of living life. Previously, they may have been denied access to their own beliefs from a young age because of more dominant family beliefs or societal beliefs, or even because of traumatic experiences. A breakdown brings to light our old, limiting structures that no longer serve us. Our higher selves work hard on our behalf to bring about healing and maintain health in our lives. The soul attempts to penetrate our consciousness, through the channel of our intuition, to send us information on how to heal, be whole, and live a life connected to the Divine. The soul never gives up on us; it is always trying to get its message through to us. A breakdown typically occurs after the soul has repeatedly tried, without success, to bring its message home to us. If subtle—or not so subtle—messaging does not get through, then a major life crisis rarely fails to leave its mark, which explains why, so often, in the wake of tragedy and crisis, people say things like: *It helped me become clear on what is important to me.*

If we can shift our perception of breakdown, it becomes easy to see that crises actually provide opportunities to listen intently to our intuition. When we do so, we become receptive to the Divine, opening ourselves to support and healing as our path takes an unexpected turn. At this pivotal juncture, Divine support comes to us in perfect order, and it behooves us to be open to the myriad forms Divine help may take. It might mean that healthier people come into our lives. Alternately, it may mean that we lose things to which we were attached, but through the loss and grief we experience, we gain appreciation for other gifts we have been given.

Not all Initial Heart Openings are breakdowns, however. In fact, some of the most beautiful heart opening experiences, such as falling in love or the birth of a child, can alter life, fill the heart with love, and still proceed Chaos. For many women, Chaos can ensue after childbirth in the form of post-partum depression or fluctuating emotions, recovery from surgery, or just simply a dismantling of expectations of how the birth should have gone. Yet a new mother can be filled with feelings of wholeness, purpose, and that life feels complete. In this case, the heart feels expanded and full of love. Love, itself, is such a powerful energy that it can lift spirits, heal mental or hormonal imbalances, and bring a sense of peace through any of life's changes.

Before I met my husband, I had one failed dating experience after another for years. I had given up on praying for the perfect partner. Instead, I started to pray for my heart to open. I had no idea who would walk in. My husband did not fit the picture of who I was looking for at the time. Yet, I was pleasantly surprised. He was Costa Rican, strong in his Latin culture, muscular, a former professional surfer, and already a father. When we first met, I saw his heart, his adorning qualities, love in his eyes, a generous spirit, and a depth that he let me in to see. It felt crazy to fall in love so quickly, but I knew he would put me first. Not that I needed him to, but he had that level of commitment in him.

A month after we met, I became pregnant. I was shocked and very afraid. It felt crazy to be having a baby with someone I had just met, yet a powerful heart energy carried us, and my intuition said, "Keep going."

The birth of my daughter blew my heart open even more. Yes, there was chaos for me after birth. We were still getting used to a new relationship, I wasn't financially prepared, I had to go back to work early, it was winter (I'm not a fan of winter), I had cabin fever and some post-partum depression, and I couldn't juggle life or feed myself very well. However, all of that was trumped by the love I felt for my daughter and my husband. He cooked and cleaned and made sure I was well cared for, which made it so much more manageable to make this major life transition into motherhood.

My experience is an example of how an Initial Heart Opening can lead to an expanded heart and prevailing love. It's a beautiful and blissful experience that can also feel crazy and non-rational. It makes you look at your life through a completely new lens. Chaos can still occur after this type of heart opening; however, the chaos is a bit more temporary because you are supported by love.

Intuition

In addition to the Higher Self or Soul, another aspect of our subconscious operating system that supports our growth and wellbeing is our intuition. Intuition is the voice of our Soul communicating to our consciousness. Some people are innately more sensitive than others, and those who are more sensitive typically tend to be more intuitive. That said, social and family frameworks can also affect the intuitive development of a human being. For example, if a family lives by the belief that credibility requires hard facts, scientific evidence, or logical reasoning, it's very probable that an individual raised in this family won't give much credence to a concept such as intuition, nor experience much in the way of soul connection. That does not mean that such a person does not have intuition. To the contrary: *everyone* has intuition. Where we differ from one another is the extent to which we have developed it so we can access and make use of it in our lives. Think, for instance, how often you have *gut feelings* about things in your life. Think, too, about all the times you didn't follow your gut and found yourself in a mess of some sort, only to discover later that if you would have done the thing you were prompted to do by that *little voice inside*, you could have avoided the mess, saving yourself time and energy.

Intuition is the internal wisdom that guides us on our path. When we are centered and clear, our energetic bodies are in alignment with Divine Grace, and intuition is very clear. When we are emotionally reactive, ungrounded, scattered, or disconnected from ourselves, our intuition is not clear or accurate. This is one reason why it is so important to clear, relax, and release emotions—so our intuitive voice can come through more clearly.

Intuition resonates differently in different power centers, or chakras,

87

in the body. In the Heart Chakra, intuition is the voice of the soul guiding us to experience ideal states of the heart, in union with the Divine. *The ideal states of the heart are: joy, love, peace, bliss, elation, and devotion. Our Soul recognizes that these true states of ecstasy happen when we are in union with the Divine; hence, intuition in the heart will draw us to experiences that afford us those feelings.* Some of us have lifetimes of karma to weed through before we can feel those states of being, while for others, such states of being are more easily accessible. Intuition in the heart is geared toward achieving the wants and desires reflected in our soul's true purpose so we can live truly meaningful lives.

When the body has physical reactions to energy around you, it is an indication of intuition activated in the Third Chakra. I refer to this as Third Chakra Intuition. Being overwhelmed, feeling spacey, having stomachaches or a spinning head are all reactions to taking in too much information through the gut. To explain this further, the Solar Plexus or Third Chakra is the power center we instinctually use to navigate through life. If we are feeling out social situations or other people's feelings, we can have a body reaction to something that does or does not feel good to us. In this power center, we need to have a clear sense of self. Otherwise, we can lose our center, absorb other peoples' energy, and put other people's needs before our own. Strong intuition requires a strong sense of self.

It also takes *intuitive guts*, i.e., determination, to follow through with our heart's mission. While we may feel a yearning for the ideal states of the heart, without the determination of a strong Solar Plexus, we may never manifest what our heart truly desires. In the period leading up to an Initial Heart Opening, we may sense, or intuitively know, what we are being called to do, but just knowing is not enough: it takes a strong sense of self, rooted in healthy internal confidence, as well as confidence in the Divine, not only to hear intuition, but also to act on it.

If intuition is ignored or denied, chaos can happen in the body and in life. When we don't listen to intuition, it means the Wounded Ego has a pretty strong grip on our psyche. The good news is that if we're hearing intuition at all, it means an opening is taking place, at which point we should turn to the wisdom of our inner voice rather than run away from its message. In an Initial Heart Opening, sometimes the heart has to crack open for us to hear our intuitive voice more clearly.

How Do I Hear My Intuition?

If you are very connected to your intuition, you will already know how wonderful it is. Continue doing what you are doing to stay connected to yourself and your inner voice.

If, however, you are new to accessing your intuition, or you are somewhat familiar with your intuitive voice but wish to strengthen it, you can:

♥ **Pay attention to the signs** and signals the universe is sending you. If life feels hard or you feel like you are swimming upstream, STOP the drive to keep pushing, and listen.

♥ **Quiet your mind** by focusing on your breath.

♥ **Bring your attention to your heart** and imagine a little child version of yourself there. Focus on listening to him or her tell you what he or she needs.

♥ **Begin trusting with small steps.** To build trust in your intuition, follow through on little gut feelings and hunches, and notice what happens when you do. The validation of seeing desired outcomes of intuitive *hunches* increases trust in your intuition, and over time, the more you listen and heed your intuition, the stronger it gets.

In addition to these suggestions, I also teach extensive workshops and trainings on developing intuition through my School of Intuitive Studies (www.SchoolofIntuitiveStudies.com), including the transformational Healer Training Program. Please visit my website for more information on education around intuitive development.

Taking It to the Next Level

The Initial Heart Opening is a period of time and state of being that takes us to the next level in ourselves. Our soul decides it's time to grow, so the heart gets bigger and stretches its boundaries. We may experience a physical sensation in our bodies or a welling up of emotion, and then, life as we know it starts to change. Our Monkey Mind will want to pull us backwards to the old and familiar ways that haven't been working for us. So what do we do? Where is our strength? To whom do we turn? This is the time when we turn inward and listen to our intuition. These are the times in life when the river is flowing, we're in a boat, and we toss the oars in the water and let our intuition guide us down the river. Life goes on. The river will always flow. It's at this point that we need to rely on our own internal strength and our intuition to be our guiding light. It will lead us to the people and the situations that will join us on our path to help us.

REFLECTION QUESTIONS

Theme:
How to Support Yourself
through an Initial Heart Opening

Step 1. Talk about your Initial Heart Opening (IHO)

Sharing your story can be cathartic. Tell or write the story of your experience: be concise, to the point, and acknowledge the feelings present for you as you experience your IHO. Finally, describe how your perspective of the experience has shifted, and what this new perspective brings you, when you think of your experience as a heart opening, rather than a tragedy.

Step 2. Consider these questions:

♥ What was my Initial Heart Opening?

♥ What lessons did I learn after experiencing an IHO? (For instance: to get connected to deeper feelings, to trust myself more, to learn how to have boundaries, to let go, to learn that life is precious and to take nothing for granted)

♥ Prior to my IHO, was my heart or my intuition trying to tell me something that I wasn't hearing or acting on? If so, what?

♥ What childhood beliefs led up to my IHO? For instance: I'm not good enough, it's not okay for me to show my feelings, etc.

♥ Do those childhood beliefs still serve me in any way? If not, what would be a new belief I could live from?

♥ What emotions arose around the situation? Did I let myself feel them?

♥ Do I need to forgive myself or someone else involved in the situation? If so, will I?

♫ **GUIDED MEDITATION AUDIO**

Log in to www.SchoolofIntuitiveStudies.com through the Expanding Your Heart link to receive your guided meditation titled "Initial Heart Opening Meditation."

Chapter 5

CHAOS

"Chaos often fosters the greatest creativity. Breakdowns often pre-cede the greatest breakthroughs. And when the pain is greatest is often when we're on the brink of the greatest realization.... When the pain is burned through rather than numbed, when our darkness is brought to light and then forgiven, then and only then can we move on. And move on we do."

— Marianne Williamson

Chaos is a state of uncertainty and dismantling that follows an Initial Heart Opening. It happens when we are living in a way unaligned with our truth, or when a deeper truth needs to be revealed. What this means is that as we undergo an initial heart opening, the parts of our being that are still wounded by past experiences—such as heart-break, accidents, or family conflicts—come to our attention, requiring scrutiny and healing. In other words, we don't just slip into a blissful Divine state of being after having an initial heart opening; *most likely, we will have to fall apart a bit further.* Some people have an easier time than others in the wake of a heart opening, but my experience has shown that revealing truths in life bring emotions to the surface. Sometimes, we get an increase in positive emotions, while more often, we are faced with challenging emotions that need to be processed and worked through.

Chaos facilitates the removal of blindfolds to truth, and it allows for an unraveling of what does not serve us. This process often brings confusion, leaving us feeling like we've been fooled by what we've previously lived. In Chaos, we might ask ourselves: Where have I been? What have I been doing? We may then encounter waves of emotion or discombobulating events of a traumatic or catastrophic nature. We may question decisions we've made. Say, for instance, you've had a major revelation that your soul's mission in this life is to garden and grow produce, but you came from a family of doctors and lawyers, where there's a pretty strong expectation that you will follow in the family's footsteps. Familial programming or expectation of any kind is not easy to walk away from because we have a deep primal bond to our original tribe, and through that bond, we've learned how to survive and excel in life. Heeding the call of your inner voice will often bring you into conflict with your past: family, relationships, schooling, jobs, etc. Making sense of, and coming to terms with, this conflict can be painful, and it is often disruptive. In other words, it is chaotic.

Chaos, in a grander sense, is the manifestation in our lives of a particular form of Divine life force. Connected to a higher intelligence, this force moves through our lives in ways we could not conceivably control. Tornados, tsunamis, hurricanes, earthquakes, and other natural disasters are forms of Divine Chaos. When they occur, they shake us to the core, uproot us, and shake our foundation, sometimes entirely shifting the direction of our lives. If, for instance, our home is demolished in a tornado, whatever we thought to be true about our stability in life completely changes. We may have to move to a new location and leave everything we've ever known. Emotions may surface uncontrollably, and we may be left with symptoms induced by trauma. We may even have had such a close brush with death that we live our lives from a completely different perspective afterwards. While disasters that are beyond reason can cause us to question our faith and trust in God or in the Universe, we have nothing to gain but harm if we actually do lose faith or relinquish trust in the Divine. Seeing Chaos as a natural part of the cycle of life can help us muster the internal stamina required to avoid being shaken to the core by Chaos.

Spiritual openings that occur during Chaos can be powerful. We start to see truth about how we feel, what we really want, who we are, who other people are, what our intuition was telling us, and what lead us to the point of unraveling. It is truth, in fact, that tends to motivate us to take the steps necessary to move through Chaos into the stage of Healing.

Chaos Happens So We Can Arrive at Truth

Tina shares her story below of how the chaos she went through helped her arrive at her truth.

Tina's Story

I was married, mother to three children, and working full-time as a paralegal/office manager in downtown Boston. I was in my mid-thirties when things became very unsettled and tumultuous within me. I began questioning my marriage and everything else about my life. My husband was an alcoholic, and I have the other part of the disease, codependency. We were away without our children one weekend, and at some point during that weekend, I absolutely knew my marriage was over. Now I understand that this was my Initial Heart Opening, which was followed by the next stage, Chaos. I've got this one mastered!

My husband and I separated, and over a two-year period, divorced. In the process of our divorce becoming final, my husband died of cirrhosis. He was diagnosed in November and was dead in December. Here I was with three children who were seventeen, fourteen, and ten. My children were still in shock over us divorcing and now their dad was dead. I went to collect a large life insurance policy and was informed that my husband had lapsed on his payment and the policy was null and void.

I returned to work part-time. One day while I was at work, in another defining moment, my oldest daughter called me, crying hysterically because she had vividly dreamt of her father. In that moment, I knew I had to leave my job and be home with my children. I said, "Okay, God; I need to turn this whole mess over to you." I was working at a bank at the time; before I left my job, I took out a $100K home equity loan since employees received special rates. For years, I lived on credit cards ($100K credit card debt) and the home equity loan, robbing Peter to pay Paul. In the midst of all of this, I had to empty and sell my husband's condo and run his business, which involved driving a truck—a big one! At this time, the financial markets crashed, leaving my home, my ex-husband's condo, and my business worth way less than anticipated. Just writing about this makes me anxious because I am flooded with the body memories of what I went through! It was an extremely difficult time. How was I going to care for my kids, emotionally and financially?

I was raised Catholic, but I had long left religion behind. At some point in this process, I began looking for relief. I found a massage therapist who was a yoga teacher and reiki master teacher. I received monthly massages, combined with reiki, to soothe myself. I attended two yoga classes and signed myself up for a teacher training program. It just spoke to my soul in such a profound way. I knew this was my path. I knew I needed to commit myself to healing my soul. I have been on that journey ever since. This whole experience resulted in my return to faith and God. That's all I had—prayer, Spirit, angels, ascended masters—you name it, I have explored and utilized it for my own healing. The more I trusted, the more my path was laid before me. From yoga teacher training, I went on to become a reiki master teacher, then off to massage therapy school. I have been studying In-Depth Body-Centered Psychotherapy and Subtle Energy Healing at Hartford Family Institute for seven years now. I have completed Wendy's Healer Training Program, and there have been many other holistic trainings and certifications—all in the name of healing myself.

Things have certainly settled down, and I have landed in myself. At a certain point, you realize the journey goes on. The heart can be opened eternally. There is always the next place to clear and open. The path becomes constantly liberating the heart—being mindful of each moment, each blessing, each opportunity to grow, learn, and serve others as they journey back to their hearts. The stages overlap; they weave from one to the other.

My experiences have brought me to my knees and humbled me beyond what words could ever convey. There have also been many magical moments and miracles along the way. I wouldn't trade any of it; it's what makes me who I am.

In Tina's story, she describes a period of chaos that she went through after her divorce and the death of her ex-husband. She also describes how amidst the chaos and financial crisis, she felt spiritually called. She found yoga teacher training and reiki to help with her healing. From there, other doors opened for her. What Tina does not say in her story is that she is a brilliant light being. She is the kind of person who glows, has so much wisdom, and is so comfortable to be around. Being connected spiritually is truth for Tina. Yet she had to go through an incredible unraveling in order to find her healing path.

Only You Can Know Your Truth

Even in the greater matrix of life and in the complexity of our physiology, Truth is at the core. While truth at this level is universal and in alignment with Divine principles of love and connection to Source, *the path to Truth remains unique to each person.* This is why, for instance, your truth about living near the ocean differs from your parents' truth that led to you being raised in a city. On the path to discovering our truth, we intuitively know what our being needs, even if it goes against the norms of our upbringing or contradicts what others want for us, or need themselves. The truth to which I am referring is not always about where to live, or whether a marriage was the right choice; sometimes, we have to practice living truth in stages to arrive at what our soul ultimately longs for. If, for instance, you make a significant sacrifice to live in a way that contradicts how you would have preferred your life to be, your intermediate truth could be acceptance of the situation. For example, you would like to move to a new state, but you may have to sacrifice that need for a few years until your partner or loved one finishes his or her degree or a job. From the plateau of acceptance, you gain a new perspective on your situation that makes it possible for you to explore further the core of your truth.

In my life, while I was called to live in a part of the country more in alignment with my Divine truth and Divine nature, when I arrived there, it wasn't the case that I kicked back in a hammock, proclaiming, "I've arrived at my final destination!" What happened is that my life began to unravel, but *I chose to stay open and conscious to the signs I was receiving.* Simply making the geographic move was not the end of the move I was taking in the direction of my heart's calling. The geographic move wasn't the whole of my truth. More was to be revealed, and I didn't lose faith in the process. I kept listening, paying attention, and practicing acceptance for what was taking place, trusting the wisdom of my calling—despite the chaos of my external circumstances.

Not living truthfully mirrors the experience of holding on to a lie, which can feel like something is eating at us, or burning in our chest. We might even feel like we're imploding—because we actually are imploding. Our most natural states of being occur when the heart is clear and we are being honest with ourselves and with others. The falsehood of holding on to, or living, a lie twists energy in the body, which then underlies everything we do. This can lead to making excuses for why we live the way we do to cover up the lie. At some point, we may feel a burning desire to talk to someone about it, and when we actually do, we might experience shame or humiliation connected to the lie we have been concealing.

How Chaos Takes Shape

Josie was the model wife and mother. She did everything imaginable for her husband and children; her whole life was dedicated to raising and caring for her family. Her husband was an elusive man, but she was aware of this characteristic when she married him. While part of her was always suspicious of his fidelity to her, she never questioned him directly about it. She felt it would be better for her and the children never to address her suspicions. Outwardly, she was valued for her ability to accomplish so much and run a wonderful household. Inside, however, she developed heart palpitations, and she began to be critical and patronizing of other people. Typically, she prided herself on the organized state of her life, but it didn't take long before the outside of her life began to mirror the internal chaos developing inside her: her house was a mess, her emotions were a mess, she was always late, and she felt constantly as if she were two steps behind. Her friends started to back away from her, and her children were confused by her changed behavior. She could not voice the burning suspicion she harbored about her husband's fidelity, so she projected it outward onto the people and circumstances in her life.

Josie ruminated on her suspicion for several more years, until one day her husband announced that he wanted a divorce. She eventually found out that he had been having an affair for years, but he didn't want to divorce while the children were still very young. Needless to say, Josie was exceedingly angry about the divorce, and her anger felt out of control; she felt out of control. She *was* out of control because she was in Chaos. Her intuition had been telling her for a long time that something was not right, but it had been her choice to remain silent about it. In truth, her anger was less about the divorce itself, and more about the fact that she had not paid attention to what her intuition was telling her, nor spoken up about it. Had she just opened up the conversation with her husband when she first felt that gut feeling, it might have afforded them an opportunity to address some deeper issues in their marriage. Even if the divorce were inevitable, she would have maintained her dignity and felt more empowered in the situation.

Josie's story exemplifies a number of the underlying factors that contribute to the internal development of Chaos, namely:

- ♥ Disconnection from Intuition
- ♥ Lack of Inner Security/Void of Spiritual Strength
- ♥ Unprocessed or Denied Emotions
- ♥ Trauma or Initial Heart Openings

Tamara Star, creator of DailyTransformations.com, shares on her website an intensely personal period of Chaos in her own life. In a thirty-day period, she endured a breakup, a lost pregnancy, financial devastation, loss of two beloved pets...(and the list goes on). You can read the full story in her blog post entitled *How to Bounce Back* (http://www.daily-transformations.com/how-to-bounce-back/). She shares not only how she overcame this incredible breakdown, but also how she grew from it. She also describes the incredible gift that comes amidst Chaos—namely, a "spark of clarity." That spark of clarity is your Divine spirit that comes through the pain of Chaos to direct you. Tamara writes the following:

When life blows up there is a crystal clarity that comes:

- ♥ All of the issues you've been hiding behind with your job or your money or your relationship are out there in the open.

- ♥ In the middle of the night, I learned to pray for help and finally learned to listen for the answer.

- ♥ And in the end, most of all I learned that when we're broken, we're really just broken open.

- ♥ I became the seed that sits in the dark, damp earth waiting for spring, deciding in which direction to send up a sprout.

- ♥ When life unravels, we're all that seed needing to trust that the darkness we're residing in, temporarily, will in the end move us towards our next fertile direction.

In moments of Chaos, windows open to our soul's clarity. Those clear moments may be hit or miss, but they are moments when our intuition is coming through to help navigate us through the Chaos. In the remainder of this chapter, I will address the roots of Chaos in the energetic body, the role of intuition in Chaos, the importance of inner security, emotions, spiritual strength, and Chaos after Trauma or an Initial Heart Opening.

Disconnection from Intuition

In my personal journey, I was so immersed in my ego and personal desires that I refused to hear my inner voice, which was telling me to go deeper into my healing work because I did not want to hear anything that told me to give up music. I did not understand that by letting go of my ego's attachment to music in order to follow the intuitive work in front of me at the time, music would eventually come back into my life in a more fulfilling way. I paid no attention to that voice and instead went through a series of catastrophes that would re-traumatize me over and over again. Eventually, I learned how crucial it is to my overall health and wellbeing to listen to my intuition and act on its wisdom. Intuition, being the voice of our soul, will always tell us the truth, *even if it's not what we want to hear.* When we don't listen to our intuition, Chaos happens. It takes a lot of courage to face the feelings we experience in the wake of challenging circumstances, but this is what helps us find truth and move through the state of Chaos. Being in tune with our actual feelings, and being honest about them, allows us to feel centered. We feel better when we are honest and acting in integrity. Chaos is where we land when we don't validate our true feelings, listen to our intuition, or have clarity about whose feelings we're feeling (ours or other people's). Chaos is not our truth, and we are not meant to live out our lives in it. We go *through* Chaos to come clean, to take an inventory of our lives, and to sort out those things that burden us in order to create space to embody more of our light and its life-affirming truth.

Our inner voice is how our soul communicates with us, and it has to pass through the chatter of the Wounded Ego. Chaos is the result of our identity being invested in things that are not in alignment with our Divine nature. For example, if our diet consists mostly of fast or processed food, it won't be long before our bodies tell us something is not right. We may feel tired, constipated, be pale, or have digestive problems. Pretty quickly, our bodies send us the signal that if we eat junk food, our health will be in Chaos. When we have a feeling that something is not right—or conversely, that something is very right—we are hearing our truth. While it is our fundamental right to live truthful lives, we are living in a time when our moods, self-esteem, and dignity are often heavily invested in material and physical perceptions of what's considered successful or socially accepted. One way of framing this idea is to understand that perception has an external, rather than an internal focus. When what we see prioritizes external influences, and we lack the inner gaze of our heart's consciousness, a veil is blocking our intuition and clouding our awareness.

Fortunately, we are now in a time of expanding Heart Consciousness, and it's truly amazing to witness the increased number of individuals seeking spiritual teachings, doing meditation and yoga, and learning about nutrition and other mindful approaches to life—all originating from an internal desire to feed the spirit. That is intuition at work. Knowing there's more to life than surface perceptions, and hearing the call to explore what that *more* might look like is intuition in action; hearing and heeding the inner call for more connection to the Soul is the work of our intuition.

Intuition is the bridge between the conscious mind and the Soul. The natural progression of our soul's evolution involves conscious expansion of our awareness. The role of intuition is to guide us truthfully through life. It is up to us, therefore, to dare courageously and fearlessly to pay attention to its calling. Sometimes, it will lead us into difficult situations because it is our karma to heal the emotions that the difficult situation brings up. In the same way that intuition can lead us into an Initial Heart Opening, it can also lead us out of Chaos and toward Healing.

While in the state of Chaos, it is our work to clear our wounds, release suppressed emotion, and fine tune our awareness in order to hear our heart's intuition guiding us. Intuition is not fortune telling; it is less concerned about the future and more concerned with your true state of being. *Intuition is about hearing what you need to know in the present moment so you are able to handle the future.*

Lack of Inner Security/Void of Spiritual Strength

When we relax in our bodies, we unwind and feel more clear and connected to ourselves. When, however, we are in an agitated emotional state, in shock, experiencing trauma, or are generally ungrounded, we describe our experience, both internal and external, as chaotic: we can't show up on time, our kids are acting up, we shut down, and we experience the demands of life as extreme. Many of us report feeling that *the demands of life are pulling us out of our center.*

The Pillar of Light

When I look at a person's energetic body, I can see when his inner energy is set deep in the core of his body. This central alignment comes from a continuous practice of self-connection, meditation, core strength, and centering practices. I can also tell when someone's energetic body has not been centered for most of his life. My gift as an intuitive enables me to see such things in the energetic body. Here is what it looks like to me: We have a central meridian in our body called the *sasumna* (pronounced shashoomna) channel. I refer to this channel as the Pillar of Light, and this pillar is our *core*. It is the main channel in our system through which life force flows. From this main channel, life force fuels all of our organs and power centers (chakras) via a network of approximately 72,000 meridians, which are pathways of energy in the body. A strong Pillar of Light tells me that someone has a strong spiritual practice, and even if this person is having an off-day, or off-month, his pillar remains strong. I can tell that whatever acute chaos he may be experiencing, he may just need some clearing and settling into his body, but he will bounce back fairly quickly because his core spiritual beliefs and his confidence in the Divine will replenish his center quickly.

On the other hand, if this pillar looks weak, is bent in certain areas, or is vacant, I know right away that the chaos happening in this person's life comes from existing wounds that prevent his willpower, or inner strength, from upholding his spirit in the face of life's challenges. For this reason, life can feel unmanageable, overwhelming, and "bombarding" to a person whose pillar is weak. In fact, when the pillar is entirely weak or weak in specific areas, external attachments are likely to prevail at the expense of internal certainty. In such cases, the person feels *insecure* instead of *secure within*. This type of insecurity can lead to an Initial Heart Opening because a person makes life choices out of insecurity, fear, and the need to feel safe, rather than from a connection to his truth. This individual makes personal investments in others, in a job, or gets attached to a house, for instance. If any of these externally validating attachments disappear, the person is devastated.

Fortifying the Pillar of Light

The Pillar of Light can be strengthened in many different ways. To begin, it is important to known that the Pillar of Light represents the Light of God within. It is an extension of our prayer channel through which our Soul communes with the Divine; therefore, spiritual practices, such as prayer and meditation, strengthen this channel in the body. Faith, courage, trust, and belief also strengthen this channel. Visualizing a waterfall of Divine Light flowing through the Pillar of Light can strengthen it. Clearing the impact of old wounding and releasing suppressed emotion and negativity clear and strengthen this channel. Yoga, acupuncture, chiropractic care, and other types of body work can heal and strengthen our pillar.

While there is not only one way to strengthen the Pillar of Light, it does require the *practice* of following your heart to find those things that are going to strengthen your connection to your Soul. Since the Pillar of Light represents your spiritual strength, ask yourself: *How am I going to strengthen my spirit so I can be a Pillar of Light in the world?* There are so many options available to you. Your way of strengthening your Pillar of Light will be unique to you, and learning to tune into your intuition will help you find the way.

By taking active responsibility for any Chaos that may exist in your life, you become the commander of your destiny. Chaos no longer *happens to you* when you choose to lean back into your Pillar of Light and observe the turmoil or confusion taking place around you; you do not fall victim to it. This doesn't mean Chaos won't touch other people, including those closest to you. While it can be challenging to witness others unwinding, or in pain, around you, it can be empowering to stand in the center of Chaos and remain centered, grounded, and calm. It is literally rewarding: *your reward for having done your work.* It means you are no longer in codependency with the Chaos; you don't have to figure out how to make it all better. When you feel the strong Pillar of Light in you, especially in difficult moments, your body is in Divine communication with Grace, and you'll know what you need to do to ride out the storm. That is a powerful feeling!

> ♫ **GUIDED AUDIO MEDITATION**
>
> I encourage you to try it. Go to the guided meditation titled "Pillar of Light" through the Expanding Your Heart Book link at www.SchoolofIntuitiveStudies.com

Chaos Can Also Lead to an Initial Heart Opening

I mentioned earlier that the stages may not happen in order. It's possible that Internal Chaos can trigger an Initial Heart Opening. One way this happens is when the Pillar of Light is weak in the body, so it's hard to establish or maintain good boundaries. This situation includes taking on others' energy or not having a very good container for our own emotions and energy, which can lead to spilling or leaking energy. I mentioned earlier how important it is to process emotions and clear old emotional energy. Repressed or unexpressed emotions show up in the energetic body as cloudy, foggy, stuck, heavy, and as energy that is not contained. Our physical bodies can only contain so much of this type of energy before it spills out, in conscious or unconscious ways. This situation can look like a person acting out, projecting emotions, crossing boundaries, or engaging in substance abuse. Chaos leads to an Initial Heart Opening when emotional energy becomes toxic in the body and the body triggers an eruption. This eruption can become an Initial Heart Opening: we crack open to purge all the unprocessed emotions, which in turn are the result of internal Chaos that has been collecting for a long time.

When Chaos triggers an Initial Heart Opening, the good news is that we are spiritually waking up. Part of this awakening has us look at what brought us to this place. We may have to face fears of letting go and open up to new beliefs, new ways of living, and new possibilities. This transformation, however, can feel like going through a warped zone after the shock of a life-changing event. Chaos then can continue after the Initial Heart Opening, until there is an honest look at, and healing for, the patterns under Chaos.

Unprocessed or Denied Emotions

Withholding emotion can create inner and outer Chaos. When emotions are not felt or dealt with, energetically they move into a person's *shadow* and become what we might call the *vibe* this person sends out. While this individual may not be dealing with her emotions, others are feeling them through the energy she is emanating. This vibe can feel toxic to others. It can also lead to the individual attracting negative experiences back into her life without understanding why this is so. Whatever is in our shadow or subconscious is part of our energy field, and the type of energy we put out to the world is the same type of energy we receive in return. Processing emotions is a way to move energy out of the shadow because we become aware of the emotions and the energy they create. Once we are aware, they are no longer a negative force that creates blocks and diverts energy to remain concealed. They are now ready to be seen, dealt with, and felt.

I know people who adamantly refuse to go to therapy because, in their eyes, therapy is for people who are crazy or who have something wrong with them. Such unwillingness to be introspective, explore one's past, or accept that there are wounds to heal are all tactics aimed at keeping the lid on a potential Pandora's Box of unprocessed emotions. Some of these people stuff their feelings down, but they keep moving through life. As I've already discussed, stuffing down emotions creates internal chaos, which in turn leads to a variety of outward expressions: cloudy thinking, memory loss, inability to make decisions, feeling stuck, projecting emotions onto others, depression, poor boundaries, heart palpitations, as well as other health problems. Our external life is a reflection of our inner state of being, so when we do not process our emotions, relationships suffer, finances suffer, home life suffers, and anything that would normally feel stabilizing starts to break down. In this breakdown, we are at last forced to feel the feelings we previously disowned. Sometimes it takes everything coming to a head in our lives for this finally to happen, but when it does, the experience ultimately leads us deeper into our soul.

The flipside to suppression of emotion is being overly emotional or dramatic. Suppression comes from a core belief that: *I can take care of myself; I don't need anyone to help me.* Being overly emotional can stem from a need for parenting in a life where emotional needs were not met as a child, resulting in a subconscious need for attention and nurturing. Interestingly enough, an overly dramatic person usually is quite good at caretaking for others and is generally generous of heart. It's very easy for her to correlate self-worth with how much she needs to take care of others, and it is common for her to give what is actually needed in any given situation. People who fit this mold feel a deep need to be loved and validated. Chaos shows up in the lives of over-givers through exploding emotions or leaking emotional energy that creates disruption and disturbance for others. This disturbance, in turn, sabotages efforts to receive the very thing such a person needs, namely love and validation. Overly emotional and dramatic behavior also shifts the burden of responsibility onto others to care-take a needy individual. Constantly having to deal with an emotionally troubled person is draining, and it strains the good-hearted intentions of friends or family members who care, but are ultimately powerless to help.

Few of us are taught at a young age that having feelings is normal, yet we all feel angry, sad, happy, excited, etc. If we can start by admitting that we may be having negative feelings, we are a step closer to accepting responsibility for such feelings, rather than projecting them onto others. *Our hurt feelings are not the responsibility of other people. Hurt feelings come from an earlier dynamic, perhaps from as far back as childhood, which is playing itself out in a particular relationship, in present time.* If you take a person with whom you are currently angry, and in your mind, you replace him or her with a parent, sibling, childhood friend, or teacher, you will be able to see in a striking manner how you are stuck in the past, trying to express in a healthy way an emotion it wasn't safe to express all those years ago. Notice all the ways your current conflict mirrors the past one, including all the emotions that are present. Though challenging to do in the moment, it might serve you to see that the conflict you now face is actually a gift that can help you become aware of, and potentially heal, the old, dysfunctional pattern of handling a particular emotion.

Trauma

When trauma occurs at a young age, Chaos may precede an Initial Heart Opening. It's possible, for instance, that a child who has endured abuse might live through a period of Chaos before arriving at opportunities for healing. Or healing may happen organically as the child grows into adulthood, facing the revealing truths about the trauma she's experienced, eventually seeking therapy to overcome its resulting impact. Healing might also happen if the trauma goes untreated and Chaos builds in the person's life to such an extent that, finally, the spirit will say, "Enough!" and an Initial Heart Opening will then take place.

What makes an event or experience traumatic, or traumatizing, is its unreasonable and disturbing nature, and the fact that, no matter how we reason, there is no making sense of it from a rational perspective. The mind cannot wrap itself around the incomprehensibility of traumatic occurrences. Try though we might, nothing makes a traumatic experience *okay*; it is too jarring, too violent. Energy and spiritual work can be especially effective in working with the impact and effects of trauma since healing the aftermath of trauma sometimes requires bypassing the rational mind to go straight to the actual stored shock and unexpressed emotions of the original event. When traumatic situations take place, many people automatically turn to the spiritual realm for answers and solace because there appear to be no valid reasons to explain what happened. While we might understand *how* things went the way they did, what we are most often seeking is an answer to our *Why?* that will make the pain go away.

When trauma takes the shape of the sudden loss of a child or loved one, or a senseless crime, it can be difficult to see these things as an opening. In fact, to someone grieving a loss, it can feel disrespectful even to consider that a light might exist in the situation. Healing trauma requires time and comfort, which is why it's important to give permission to ourselves or to our loved ones to be exactly where we are with our feelings. For example, it is reasonable to say that losing a child is not something a grieving parent needs to reconcile herself to, especially if the loss happens in a senseless way. What I'm saying is: Rather than searching for reasons to be okay, don't try to *or* strive to be okay! Let it be what it is: Be okay with the fact that the loss is not okay, which is the truth of the situation at the moment. Grief requires spaciousness and self-acceptance in order to express itself; we have to give ourselves permission to grieve. No explanation will ever take away the pain of a sudden loss. When time has passed, perhaps there will be peace, but until that time, feeling the grief and anger is what we should be doing.

How can a sudden loss be a major heart opening? Our lives are touched by everyone we know, and even by people we don't know. While you have most likely not met the Dalai Lama, for instance, your compassionate heart may be touched by his compassionate heart as it comes through to you via his teachings. Our lives are also touched by the spiritual gifts of the people we have intimately known. When a soul leaves a body, it leaves the impact of its spiritual light. The souls of the departed continue to change lives after they leave the planet: they have impact, and they propel change in the lives of those they leave behind. Sometimes, a soul that came to earth to shed light on us is so big that its light prevails long after it has passed. This is the experience we have, for example, with artists, authors, musicians, and thought leaders whose art, music, words, and ideas have posthumous resonance.

The power of a soul's impact on this world is a gift. Every soul has an incredible amount of potential to shine light and goodness, leave a positive mark on the world, and influence the lives of others. Those who have passed from our lives, whom we love and miss dearly, have also touched our hearts to such an extent that, following their departure, we view life differently, which may cause us to open up to living in a new way, making changes in our lives, advocating for truth, and, not least, honoring the precious nature of life.

A major heart opening can also result from prolonged grief or feeling that you have lost someone who is living; such cases would include the grief of the parent of a missing child or grief felt for a loved one who has fallen deeply into addiction. Whether someone dies or is removed from our life, the feeling of loss can be extremely difficult because our heartstrings to our loved ones may still be intact. Even if the loved one has not passed on, the potential for survivor's guilt is high. If you are living in loss and grief, you are feeling your heart.

Unfortunately, you are feeling pain in your heart, but you also are connecting to your heart's immense capacity to love. If you didn't love, you wouldn't feel the loss of it.

Below, Susie shares her story of how she dealt with the loss of her daughter to addiction.

Susie's Story:

When we first learned about our oldest child's addiction, I thought it was something we could fix. After all, my husband and I were competent, intelligent, and compassionate people who had, up until this point, experienced success in manipulating life to fit our desires. I thought if we could find the right school, medication, therapist, rehab center, etc., all would be well and our family would heal. It took twelve long years of chaos, heartbreak, and sorrow for me to accept that this progressive and often fatal disease was here to stay.

The realization that we, as loving parents, were not enough to find a cure for our daughter's illness drove me to look deep inside my broken heart for spiritual connection. The loss of all my hopes and dreams for my precious child has taught me to live in current space time. Chaos creeps back in when I try to make sense of the past or invest too much in future expectation. I've found peace in the present moment when I am truly open and accepting to what is.

On the rare occasion when I have the opportunity to spend time with my daughter, I try to meet her in a neutral place: physically, emotionally, and spiritually. Non-judgment allows me to see and accept her for how she truly is, and in turn, to see and accept myself more accurately. In moving past the ego blocks and directly to heart-centered love, I can allow space for God's grace to flow.

Amidst all the sadness and fear, it is a beautiful place to be, and I cherish those moments. I am so very grateful to be able to look into her deep brown eyes, hold her hand, share a hearty laugh, or embrace her with a hug. This is where I find Divine Love.

Susie lived through periods of Chaos, but she also found some solace in her spiritual heart when the situation felt helpless. It was hard for Susie to live in perpetual loss. Her daughter was alive, but self-destructive. Susie could never feel settled because the worry was so tremendous. She was heartbroken, and what worked for Susie was to go into her heart even more, to explore the pain and the spiritual opening. As Susie learned more about addiction as a disease, she was able to connect with others who have had children or loved ones who have suffered from addiction. She learned she was not alone and that addiction is an illness. This helped her let go a bit more and even see how one day she might be able to help others who have experienced a similar loss.

Loss is a heart opening because the amount of heart energy that not only flows out of us, but is also received by us from others, is an entirely non-verbal, energetic exchange that constitutes a profound and deeply-felt spiritual experience. In the event of sudden loss in your life, the stage of chaos that follows requires you to express exactly what you feel, with full compassion and acceptance for where you are in the process. *Give yourself comfort, and accept comfort from others. Grieving takes time, and honoring that time is the most compassionate way to move through the stage of Chaos.*

Moving Through Chaos

Moments of ungroundedness are not the same as a period spent in

Chaos. If we are experiencing an extended period of chaos due to life path changes, it's important to keep in mind that we are dismantling the old and creating the new. As structures are coming apart and shifting in our lives, it may be necessary to have a healthy support system around us, especially to help point us in the direction of a spiritual practice. This type of support system might include: visiting a place of worship or spiritual practice; practicing yoga; seeing a therapist, spiritual director, or healer; relying on family; connecting with a like-minded community; having a creative outlet; or following a health regimen. Having structured support can help us focus in the direction of our heart instead of distracting us from it.

If we do not make use of this time to go inward, to access our Divine connection, and to discover what our heart is calling us to do, states of Chaos can traumatize us over and over again until we realize they are a necessary catalyst meant to bring about a much-needed transformation in our lives. This means when we do look inward, we have to be willing to look at our energetic blocks (which include held emotions) instead of running from them. Not looking at our blocks can keep us stuck in Chaos because during Chaos, energy blockages we have held inside come to the surface, and they need our attention. At this point, we are presented with a clear choice: Continue to walk around wounded, or step up and take this opportunity to heal.

Here are a number of supportive steps you can take to make it through the challenging moments of Chaos:

1. Slow down.
2. Try not to make any major decisions when you are ungrounded or overly emotional.
3. Open yourself up to *going with the flow* rather than needing to know what the outcome of your situation will be. You may need

to ride out the storm to see what will show up for you. If being patient is difficult, call on your faith, and trust to the extent you are able that everything is in divine order.

4. If a decision needs to be made, then make one! (But not when you feel unstable; see #2 above.) Sometimes, simply making a choice will shift the energy in a situation. If you really don't know what choice to make, go with what you feel compelled to do. Try not to over-think it! Over-analyzing will often make Chaos worse.

5. Trust. Be open.

6. Meditate. Chant a mantra or affirmation to shift the energy. Turn inward.

Try this meditation:

Even though everything in your life is crumbling, and there is no one who can make your struggle go away; even though you're exhausted, you still have enough energy to sit in stillness. Come and rest in the temple of your heart. Take off your shoes. Sit in stillness. Feel your soul as a small version of you walking into your Heart; close the temple doors behind you. Take some deep breaths. Here, you are alone in the halls of your Sacred Heart. Sit quietly and breathe. Slow down your pace and quiet your mind until your breath becomes the loudest thing in the room. Listen to the whispering of your soul. Sit in stillness until this whispering becomes louder than the thoughts in your mind. Be here. Breathe. Cry if you need to. Feel a waterfall of light pour down to your heart. Let it wash over you, dissolving the feeling that you are alone in your situation. You are not alone. Let the light of the Divine keep you company, and between you and God, commit to meeting here again, every day. Be here for as long as you need. Each day you can release a little bit more, let a little more unfold, allow a little more to be revealed. When you are complete, give thanks for something in your life. Letting God know you appreciate what you have been given shows that you have accepted the life you have been given, even in the challenging times.

When Chaos happens, your personal structures come apart, and everything you counted on as reliable becomes uncertain. All the attachments you had previously grounded into to help you feel safe and secure can no longer hold you up. When we are invested in an external, materially based sense of security and lack internal security, it can feel like the rug is being pulled out from under us when the systems we have relied on crash down around us. We tend to take things very personally in Chaos, not being able to imagine why it is happening to us. *It happens to us because it happens to everyone.* The truth is that Chaos, and its consequent dismantling of the life we thought we were going to live, teaches us to *reset our priorities* so we can build a relationship via the heart to the Divine. The state of Chaos is an opportunity to go inside to reflect, do our inner work, accept our lives as they are, and admit failures as well as accomplishments; it is a time to face our demons and open ourselves to prayer.

Chaos is a time when it can feel like your hands are tied behind your back because, despite having read every book, tried every therapy, and exhausted your friends by telling them the same story over and over again, in the end, what you're left with is the fact that what you once thought to be reliable and true is no longer real for you. This unreal place is actually perfect. Yes, perfect—because you are just where you need to be so you can turn inward in silence and begin to pray. When your whole world is in pieces at your feet, and you can't understand why, meditation, contemplation, and prayer are more important than ever.

Sometimes, Chaos indicates that the spiritual, emotional, and physical opening is happening all at the same time. It can look like anxiety, depression, physical reactions in the body, and more. Below, Beth explains how her inner emotional chaos manifested in her life as panic and other physical conditions. She also shares how her invocation of the Divine resolved the chaos and helped her find peace.

Beth's Story

When I turned thirty-two, I was thrown into chaos physically, mentally, and emotionally. The body symptoms were extreme pain (ribs, stomach, gall bladder, liver, etc.), panic, nightmares, and whole body muscle aches to name a few. I was convinced I was dying; with all this pain, I must have a disease. I went to see every specialist possible. Why couldn't anyone figure out what was wrong with me? Surely my body was turning on me. I had no desire to eat, and whatever I managed to get into my mouth did not stay in long enough to be swallowed.

One day, I had to ask a coworker to drive me home from work because I was suffering from panic. My blood pressure was high and my pupils were extremely dilated. I was in a fog, frozen with flashes of childhood trauma surfacing. When we turned into my driveway, I was feeling as if nothing were real, and I realized I needed some help before I went crazy. As I walked into my house, my thoughts turned to the Bible. Since I was raised Catholic, growing up, we had always had a Bible in the house, so, of course, I had one in my house. The funny thing was that I had never even opened a Bible in my life, but I decided I would retrieve it from the dusty shelf. There *had* to be something I could read/focus on that would release me from this terror. I took the book out onto the back porch and laid down on the porch, sobbing all over the leather cover. Each tear raced down my cheeks,

soaking the pages with my overwhelming distress and desperation. "Please," I begged, "make this suffering go away."

I must have fallen asleep on the Bible, and when I woke, I sat
up to find myself surrounded by six deer. They seemed to be
as amazed as I was as they stood very still, gently blinked, and
walked silently into the woods. At that moment, I knew there
was a grand plan for me. Those deer were a gift, whispered
words of encouragement, a magnificent comfort, presented in
a way that *only* an animal spirit could be. God had heard my
anguish and sent the most beautiful, peaceful, furry messengers
to hold me energetically, validating and supporting me through
my struggle. It gave me a connection, a morsel of hope that God
and I could do this together.

Later that day, I went to my son's bus stop. He was in first grade
and would be bouncing off the bus in five or ten minutes. Again,
the overwhelmed feelings were back. I was unable to keep any
food down, feeling anxious with crippling abdominal pain and
terrified that things were never going to improve for me. It was
a gloomy day that mirrored my present state of mind perfectly.
At that moment, I felt as if I didn't have a thing to lose—everything was falling apart anyway; I was desperate. I felt completely open, raw, and vulnerable, but receptive.

I sat down on the curb at the end of the street and started to cry,
wondering whether I would ever again feel good a day in my
life. I sat with my head in my hands, and as I lifted my face
skyward, I said out loud, "I don't think I can handle this; this is
too much for me, God. You need to help me." As I completed
my statement, I sat very still, eyes closed, face lifted toward the
sky. Just then, the sun, a glorious most beautiful golden warmth,

surrounded my face in the most gentle, loving holding—words cannot adequately describe this deep feeling of peace and love—feeling as if God were cradling my face in His hands. I wept, but this time with the sensation of being held, free from worry, pain, and sorrow. This sensation lasted for a couple of minutes. All I could say was, "Yeah, okay. I get it."

I dried my tears and felt a sense of calm, of partnership. This was yet another magical gift! Two in one day! Letting me know I am supported, I am loved, and that spirit is guiding me. I couldn't help but notice that the grass was the deepest green I had ever seen. How did it get that way? How long had it looked like that? The singing of the birds felt like it was just for me—a private concert! Did the birds learn a new song? My thoughts shifted from "This is too much. I don't want to be here" to "I exist, and I am so grateful."

Before my heart broke open, I was not trusting of anyone. I lived in a state of constant anxiety with only anti-anxiety medication for relief from overwhelming feelings and memories of my stifled childhood existence. I felt frantic and disconnected, just going along on autopilot and wondering whether anyone really knew what a mess I was inside.

In my darkest time of need, my body was not betraying me or adding to my woes. My physical self could not remain quiet any longer—attending to my physical symptoms, yielding/surrendering to the anxiety, depression, anorexia, panic, chronic pain, nightmares, etc. was what was needed. I had to sit with each and every feeling that rose up to be acknowledged, rather than send them packing like I had always done. Giving *all* of my feelings "floor time" has kept me physically, emotionally, mentally, and spiritually healthy. It is not an easy task to trust that the universe has your back, that if you surrender to the chaos in your head, you won't lose your mind or go crazy.

Now I live my life every day knowing the importance of connecting to Divine Source throughout the day. I express gratitude for my gifts and commitment to my intuitive knowledge, and I notice how listening and yielding to a higher wisdom honors who I am, moving me closer to my true soul. I have made the conscious choice to allow Divine Source to guide me. My Higher Self/Soul wants me to merge with the magnificence that is *me*; this makes me smile. I have received some powerful messages regarding the level of support available to me, to all of us, if we just *allow*. My journey, thus far, has taken me on several interactive tours through Initial Heart Opening, Chaos, Healing, and Contemplative Being. With each cycle, I retrieve lost parts of myself, and I ask for and receive support and guidance to comfort me during the trying Chaos and to celebrate with me when I land on my feet. Each time my heart cracks open, the light comes through a little brighter and stronger.

Beth shares how she found her connection to the Divine to support her moving out of Chaos. In the questions at the end of this chapter, explore how you have experienced Chaos in your life and how you moved through it. If you are in it now, what do you need to support you in moving through Chaos?

REFLECTION QUESTIONS

Theme:
How to find your center and move through Chaos

Step 1. Talk about or reflect upon what Chaos looked like for you following an Initial Heart Opening (IHO). A great deal of clarity about the situation can be gained by understanding that your experience was a chaotic but purposeful state through which you had to pass to gain a sense of who you are. As you share or write in a journal on this topic, be concise, to the point, and acknowledge the feelings that were present for you at the time. If any emotions are still present for you about the past, name those emotions. Then listen to the audio recording to help you ground and center the feelings and energy of chaos.

To guide you from Chaos to clarity, consider the following questions to help you gain insight into how you got through Chaos, or how you can move through Chaos now if you are currently experiencing it.

Step 2. Moving from Chaos to Clarity

- ♥ Did you experience Chaos in your life following an IHO?
- ♥ If so, what did Chaos look like for you?
- ♥ How did you move out of Chaos, or did you?
- ♥ Did Chaos precede an IHO? If so, in what way?
- ♥ Thinking back, did you have any anchors or saving graces during Chaos that helped you stay grounded, such as a person, hobby, or safe place to go?
- ♥ Considering that Chaos helps us find our inner voice/intuition if we slow down enough to hear it, was there a time when you did hear your intuition? Did you listen to it? Explain.
- ♥ How did/does going through Chaos help you?

♥ Consider patterns in your life that leave you feeling chaotic. Name at least three that come easily to mind.

♥ Knowing what you know now, how would you shift these patterns to serve you better?

♥ Are you still harboring anger toward someone from your past? If so, how does that contribute to Chaos in your present?

♥ Are you ready to forgive yourself and/or others?

♥ Do you let yourself feel your feelings when they arise? If not, why?

♥ Are you aware of a particular emotion, or several emotions that you need to allow yourself to feel at this time? If so, name the emotion/s.

♥ Will you let yourself feel the emotion/s now?

♥ Considering your life today, would you say you are unconsciously creating Chaos at this time? If so, in what ways?

♥ Reflecting on the fact that happiness has to come from within, and that being peaceful and feeling content belong to the experience of happiness, notice what happens in your body when you consider this. Ask yourself: Do I experience contentment as something positive and desirable, or as something negative?

♥ If Chaos is a stage you have already moved through, how did you get through it?

♥ Did you experience a specific moment of clarity that helped you get connected to yourself?

♥ If you tune into your Soul, what would your Soul tell you to do at this time to move through Chaos?

♫ **GUIDED MEDITATION AUDIO**

Log in to www.SchoolofIntuitiveStudies.com through the Expanding Your Heart link to receive your guided meditation titled "Grounding Through Chaos Meditation."

Chapter 6

HEALING

"The soul always knows what to do to heal itself.
The challenge is to silence the mind."

— Caroline Myss

Many people will use the word *healing* with great caution because the definition of "to heal" contains the word *cure*. The medical field sounds alarms at claims of illnesses being *cured* in ways that defy scientific explanation. To be clear, when I talk about *healing*, I'm referring to a transformational process that makes use of spiritual development, increased awareness, and complementary health regimens to bring about ever increasing states of wellbeing. It is my experience that physical healing is possible through transformation of the inner state.

Over the course of many years offering energy healing in my private practice, I have seen people heal the wounds created in their pasts. As a clairvoyant and intuitive healer, I have witnessed people shift from living entirely without faith to embracing the spiritual in their lives— that is healing. I have seen people transform their physical bodies by shedding excess weight, as well as releasing what probably feels like tons of old, unexpressed emotion—that, too, is healing. I have watched people open their hearts to find joy, and I have been amazed to see individuals have completely new, transformative responses to memories or situations that once triggered an adverse reaction in them. All of this is healing.

When I first realized I was intuitive and could see energy, I knew I could use my gift to be a psychic. There is nothing wrong with working as a psychic, and being intuitive does include psychic "seeing." The metaphysical world is fairly vast, and any number of avenues were open to me as a gifted clairvoyant. But being a psychic or clairvoyant doesn't always include *healing*, and I knew that healing, specifically, was how I could best use my abilities. My calling urged me to use my abilities and acquired skills to help people clear energy and connect to the Divine for the purpose of healing. As a healer, I will never offer psychic information to anyone without also offering tools to make use of that information and bring about transformation. I have helped people transform, grow, and heal lifelong wounds, and they have reported feeling like whole new people as a result.

Is healing always an entirely positive experience? In the end, yes; it is transformative, which is positive. But healing is a journey that can be messy, challenging, and painful; it will often lead us into dark tunnels, whose lighted ends we may not perceive for long periods of time. During those dark, challenging moments, Chaos and Healing tend to exist simultaneously. Healing works in conjunction with Chaos and does not necessarily start when Chaos ends because there are no specific boundaries around the two. Rather, they work hand-in-hand. Healing can bring up Chaos, and Chaos can bring about healing. Spiritual healing is an ongoing process in life, which gets its momentum from your choice to grow personally. Absent Healing and

Chaos, there is no way to grow and evolve as a soul because both of these stages support us in taking responsibility for our actions. We are responsible for our healed or unhealed wounds and projections. Through taking responsibility, we can move out of Chaos into Healing and from Healing into a transformation.

Chaos and Healing allow unhealed wounds to come to the surface so they can be dealt with and reconciled. Often (remember, it's not always linear), the experience of Chaos has stirred up emotions and exposed deeper wounding, after which the process of healing begins. Having awareness of or understanding a particular wound, without healing it, is itself a form of Chaos. Healing takes place once we become conscious of our wounding *and* establish an intention to change. We have to be willing to change our lives for the better. If I ask you, "Do you want to be healthy and happy?" your answer most likely would be: "Yes, of course, I do!" It's amazing, though, how many of us actually *fear* feeling joy, not least because we become comfortable living with our wounds. Our entire life might conform to our particular set of wounds. If there is a wound of neglect and alcoholism, an individual's life will revolve around using alcohol to fill the deep void created by neglect by others or neglect of oneself. Everyone around this person suffers until the person becomes willing to change.

Healing is the process of taking responsibility for transforming the impact of past experiences (especially struggles) and blocked emotions that remain in the body and create separation from Source. *Healing requires a full body, mind, and soul commitment to facing fears, making changes, and growing as a person.* Because healing is a gradual process, it does not happen overnight, and no two people with similar issues heal at the same rate. All of us have a complex mapping of life experiences that contributes to who we are now. It takes patience and willingness to look at what arises emotionally, psychologically, and spiritually as we take on past wounding.

It's important to mention that even if your history was difficult and painful, your soul has the ability to heal and transform your relationship to the past. The more work we are willing to do in our lives, the more healed we become. When we clear the blocks in our system, we are literally letting go of the old, dark, negative, and limiting, and instead, taking in the light, beautiful, peaceful, loving energy of the Divine. We actually make more room in our system for our bright soul to shine. So the more healed we become, the more our being is able to embody Divine Light.

Becoming aware of our *stuff* as it comes up is a lifelong process, but as we become more comfortable and skilled at looking at our particular issues, we find that we heal more quickly. As we heal, we build personal strength and spiritual stamina, which makes it increasingly easy to manage other issues that may arise. Healing from an energetic perspective is powerful, fulfilling, challenging, and courageous.

This spiritual approach to healing bolsters healing of physical illnesses, too. Tracy Maxwell is the author of *Being Single, with Cancer*. She has told her story on the Katie Couric show and through presentations she does all over the country. Here she recounts her process of healing, from the perspective of the Four Stages:

Tracy's Story

Cancer opened my heart the most. I definitely did not anticipate that would happen when I first heard the words from my doctor. I was terrified, and then I was bitter that I would miss the glorious Colorado summer and my time as a river guide while recovering from surgery and having drugs pumped into my veins.

Interestingly, I was never angry about getting cancer—just about enduring the seemingly endless treatment. I never asked, "Why me?" Even through the most challenging, frustrating, lonely, and scary parts of my experience, I sensed there was a purpose to all of this.

The Chaos period lasted a number of years through various surgeries and treatments, follow-ups, emotional roller coasters, two recurrences, lots of reading and research and discovering new treatment paths. It also enveloped all my relationships, my career, my finances, and forced me to consider, almost daily, my own mortality and the reason I was put on the planet to begin with.

When I really embraced the healing part of my illness, and other life traumas since, I got that cancer was just a symptom of a bigger problem. It was really the patterns in my life—emotionally, mentally, physically, and spiritually—that weren't serving me. Cancer was a glorious wake-up call to get me to make some major changes in all of the above. I learned so much—primarily and most importantly, to allow myself to ask for and receive help. It would have to be something as serious as cancer to get me to do that. A broken ankle in the middle of a Colorado winter, on crutches with outside stairs and not being able to drive six years previously, hadn't done it.

I uncovered a belief system about my value (or lack thereof) that tied my worth to what I was able to give. As a result, for years, I had been giving way more than I received, and taking responsibility (emotionally, if nothing else) for the problems in my family, my company, my friends, and really, the world. I gave until I didn't have anything left, and then I began digging into my own reserves to give some more. This just left me depleted. If my value were connected to what I gave, how much do you think I asked for help? Yeah, not so much. Not only would I not be a contribution, I thought; I would be a burden.

Enter cancer. I could not have gotten through seven years of health issues, financial struggles, starting and running my own nonprofit, being single and living alone without significant help. The minute I was able to be vulnerable enough to request help and allow it in, help showed up in droves in the form of emotional support, caregivers, donations, treatment recommendations, programs, cleaning, meals, rides, a mountain of cards, gifts, hats/scarves, and so much more. It is still not easy for me to ask for help or to see that I have value beyond just what I contribute to others, but now when the old patterns emerge, I recognize them right away and deal with them quickly without getting mired in the muck.

Now, I help others heal their own patterns through speaking, coaching, leading retreats and healing trips, and through my book *Being Single, with Cancer: A Solo Survivor's Guide to Life, Love, Health, and Happiness.* I see cancer as a huge gift that helped me heal. I am grateful for it.

Tracy demonstrates that when a physical crisis happens in the body, such as cancer, it forces a deeper look at what thoughts, feelings, and patterns exist in order to heal from the illness. What is important to know here is that under every physical illness, there is an energetic component because our body is made up of energy. The treatment, however, may not always be cured by energy healing. In fact, once an illness such as cancer manifests, there may be many different treatments to help shift the cells in the body. Those treatments can range from alkalining the body through diet to surgery. In this case, Tracy describes that cancer inspired her process of spiritual awakening and healing. Healing for Tracy wasn't just about curing cancer. It was about the personal and spiritual transformation she was about to go through as a result of having cancer.

Why Do We Heal?

"Why do we heal?" is a foundational question that underlies the path of our soul on the planet. As souls, we are born from Divine Light, and we return to Divine Light. Our fundamental gift is to have a body here on planet Earth. Our service to the Divine is to live our fullest potential in this body and in this life, and to contribute back to life by means of expressing our unique gifts.

Innately, we want to give and receive love, experience overall wellbeing, know trust, feel safe and secure, and live in happiness. As a result of our karma or current life experiences, it may be the case that we are at peace with ourselves, or we have a hard time feeling good, safe, and happy as a result of restrictive belief systems or confining imprints from life experiences.

We heal with the support of an invisible current within us that brings us ever closer to our internal light. Some call this current Grace. Whether we know it or not, our inner intelligence is constantly guiding us closer to the light. We may perceive Grace's urging as an internal knowing that we have more energy available to us than we are currently accessing. This idea that more is available to us might apply to our career, or love life, or even our ability to feel happy.

However counterintuitive it seems, we don't grow through being comfortable. We grow through hitting our edge: being challenged by relationships, in particular, but also by other life circumstances. As we grow and evolve, we are presented with life experiences that provide opportunities for us to heal the unfinished business of our past so we can experience the full potential of our spirit in this lifetime. We are also creating opportunities to listen to our intuition and to live more in truth and in the light of who we are.

So, as we evolve personally, life experiences present opportunities for us to heal the past so we may know the full potential of our spirit in this lifetime. We are also creating opportunities to live more in truth and in the light of who we are.

Not everyone lives up to his or her fullest potential because of different levels of consciousness. To clarify, if a person is unaware of his own wounds, he may not have the consciousness that healing exists for him. Potential is, therefore, limited by how much awareness there is. However, there is no hierarchy to consciousness due to each person's individual ability to have his own unique path and ways that he contributes to life. It may be my path to write a book and bring light to people that way, but it could be a baker's path to bring joy and light to others through baking. We may have a different consciousness around our intentions, yet we are both operating from genuine goodness to offer our hearts to others.

Unfortunately, not every person has the feeling that goodness is at his or her core. Some people are plagued with suffering that may inflict pain on others. This suffering includes a lack of heart or lack of empathy. This kind of person could be a serial killer, rapist, or criminal. I'm not suggesting that every criminal feels he is bad at his core. I cannot speak for others' feelings. Deep injury, however, has internal demons that prey on its supply of dark feelings. In these dark moments, it is difficult to access innate goodness. It's not that these people cannot heal, but healing may have to begin on a soul and spiritual level so they can build new values to sustain working through issues psychologically.

Yet every one of us has some level of anger, rage, war, loneliness, despair, hopelessness, and self-criticism that pops up somewhere in our lives. So it is our responsibility as spiritually progressing souls to transform the pain within us, in order to heal our contribution to pain on the planet. Healing is about transforming the darkness within us so we may:

♥ Become Light
♥ Find Truth
♥ Know God and the Divine within us
♥ Be Free from pain and suffering

We heal because it is part of our soul's evolution here on this Earth to learn, grow, and raise consciousness, not for ourselves only, but for the collective. As we continue to grow and vibrate at higher frequencies, we teach others to do so just by example, and we learn from others who are shining light on us. Our lives change the more we operate within these higher levels according to our innate nature to do good and to be good.

By vibrating at a higher frequency, I refer to energy's different levels of vibration. Lower frequency vibrations could be anger, rage, fear, and greed. Higher vibrations include love, peace, generosity, and joy. We are complex human beings because we carry a spectrum of all these emotions within ourselves at any given moment. Our reactions to present situations are often influenced by past experiences, and they can bring up any one of these emotions. Whether or not our past was filled with difficulty or with ease, our Soul is driving us toward healing, which could bring up the lower frequency emotions. The more we heal, the higher our frequency becomes. When we move through anger, for example, peace could be on the other side of it. We may feel lighter to ourselves and others. That is vibrating at a higher level of consciousness.

As we heal ourselves, we demonstrate a model for healing that teaches others. Sometimes, it's not even taught verbally; we may simply emanate a vibration that people gravitate toward and want to feel in themselves. In this way, we are raising consciousness.

On the other hand, we often revert to negative thoughts. These thoughts may continuously infuse into your day-to-day thinking so you never realize they create suffering. Take this thought, for example: "I have so much to do today that I don't know how I'm going to get it all done." This thought is actually creating suffering. It implies that the body is in a state of stress due to too many strings or attachments. There is no room for peace when in this way of thinking. (Believe me; I know this one!) If this is a perpetual thought, then perhaps it is necessary to analyze why you are packing so much into one day. Shifting schedules, delegating tasks, or evaluating the importance of the tasks could relieve this suffering. The excuses we use in relation to any of these solutions range from "But I can't shift my schedule because then I'll let someone down" to "If I don't do it, nothing will get done." In this moment, your Wounded Ego is telling you there is no room for you, and others' needs are more important than your own. The spiral downward of useless sufferings has begun.

Ideally, humanity seeks happiness. Yet, we are engorged by self-punishment that keeps us from the discovery of that true inner joy. Healing requires taking note of when you are in a low frequency of negative thinking and negative feelings. When you are in a low frequency, it is possible that you are not getting something you are needing on a deeper level. For example, you may need to feel comfort, feel heard, find joy, take a break, or have some time for yourself.

Your frequency will shift as you tune into yourself and connect to a deeper need. Tuning into yourself does require practice. If you are just beginning to practice tuning in to your intuitive voice, then it will take practice before it becomes a thought in your conscious mind to check in with yourself. Make it a practice, though. Most of the time, people look to others to meet a deeper soul need, and they get disappointed when people can't satisfy that need. So become familiar with tuning into yourself and asking your own body, mind, and soul what you need when you are in a state of upset. This introspection will help you become more conscious to your part in shifting your vibration.

Raising your vibration may be a process in itself. As mentioned earlier, when we take responsibility for the emotions we feel, and we feel them, they move out of the shadow and into the light. They are no longer creating a low vibration. Bringing them to light will clean the vibration around you. Experiencing your own light shows that your soul is evolving. That is a part of spiritual growth. Any time you are growing and healing, it raises your vibration; you then become filled with light.
We heal in order to expand our soul, raise consciousness within us and for the planet, and to become more spiritually connected. As a result, our life changes, our relationships change, our habits change, and we have the opportunity to experience the potential energy with which we came into this world.

Practice in Shifting Vibration: What would it feel like to have tea or coffee with a person who is happy, pain-free, successful, and unconditionally supportive of you? If you do not have that person in your life, why not attract that person into your life? How? What if you became that person?

Here's how: Accept that there is a higher vibrational frequency of living. It includes thinking positively and appreciating your life and everyone in it—friends and enemies. Then close your eyes and imagine that this cargo of your sufferings is being loaded onto a barge and floating out to sea. (How about throwing the really heavy baggage off a cliff?) Now imagine that your body is separated at the waist by a northern and southern hemisphere. The southern hemisphere holds islands of fear, resentment, anger, and hatred. Let us call that your *suffering spiral*. The northern hemisphere encompasses the horizons of love, joy, generosity, illumination, and truth. I will refer to these as your *higher frequency*. Now feel your feet on the ground. Visualize the suffering spiral escaping your body and falling down a long tube into the earth's center. Breathe deeply as you visualize. It may take ten minutes or more for the energy to clear. Then feel the higher frequency energy pour down into the space where the sufferings used to be. Simultaneously, your body pulsates with a glow of light. Your feet are still grounded, but the illumination from your heart also emanates to the lower half of your body. Fill yourself up with golden light! Feel it radiate in all directions.

Examine next how you treat the people you know. Do you complain to them? Do you commiserate with their sufferings? Do you need them to talk to you about your problems? Notice whether your relationship has been built on keeping sufferings alive. Choose higher frequency ways of relating to others. For example: Tell them you love and appreciate them; choose to do more fun activities in your own life or with others; see the goodness in others' efforts, even if you have been disappointed by their actions in the past. Remember, you can only do this life once, and we all have the ability to change our thoughts in order to raise our frequencies.

Raising consciousness includes letting go of the relationships, addictions, toxins, and negative habits keeping you in a lower frequency. Sometimes, it takes eliminating these major attachments and enduring the process it takes to unravel from this kind of suffering spiral (which may include therapies or outside support). Choose to surround yourself with happier people and joyful experiences, and allow them to teach you how to transform into their reflections. Sometimes, the Divine sends us messages and signs that help us grow and persevere on our path. As you bask in the light and positivity that these people radiate, know that you have attracted them into your life because you also have sparked an interior light.

How Do We Heal?

Healing can happen in various ways. Since spiritual and energy healing are more my expertise, I will spend more time offering information in these areas. However, a therapeutic approach to healing also may be necessary. Although I am not a therapist, I do promote the value of therapy and therapeutic techniques. Luckily, in this day and age, there is a blending of traditional therapy with alternative healing and meditation, which is a tremendous benefit to the greater good of personal growth. Both traditional therapy and energy/spiritual healing are effective in different ways. Success in healing may also depend on the practitioner or therapist, not just in his or her skill base. That includes how much the person can bring Divine Light through his own being for true healing to happen on the soul-level.

Traditional Therapy's Role in the Healing Stage

Traditional therapy or talk therapy is visiting with a licensed and trained therapist to talk through your personal issues, life, challenges, family systems, symptoms, etc. One way the Healing process begins is by looking at the wounds in your life, talking about them, seeing how your family history plays a role, and processing your emotions or life situations. For some people, just talking can be therapeutic and very cathartic. Big healing can happen by expressing truth out loud to someone who is skilled in hearing you. A great deal of healing can occur through revelations about your past. You will also gain perspectives that you may not have thought of before. A therapist can also help through the difficulties of being in the emotions and give you tools to be with your feelings on your own. Whether you are new to working on yourself or just prefer traditional therapy, it may take several tries to find the right therapist for you, but luckily, we live during a time when the evolution of psychotherapy provides more options than it used to, and that includes a variety of therapists.

If you have never cracked the door on looking at your past, it's possible that finding a therapist after an Initial Heart Opening or when in Chaos is a perfect step. Revelations can occur in understanding your family history, which may have developed your family structures and past experience. This knowledge allows your mind to reason out why things happened the way they did. There is value in that.

Traditional talk therapy does not typically address the soul or spiritual side of your being. Yet, nowadays, many "traditional" therapists take independent study to learn about the soul, meditation, somatic healing, energy healing, and spiritual work.

Dr. Dori Gatter, Ph.D., is a therapist, facilitator, and program director at the Hartford Family Institute in West Hartford, Connecticut. The Institute provides therapeutic trainings that include emotional and spiritual healing. She helps hundreds of people transform using traditional therapy combined with spiritual and meditative practices. In an interview I had with Dr. Dori, she explained to me how her story relates to the Four Stages.

Dr. Dori's Story

I don't know that there's any one event or trauma that opened me up. What I can say is that my entire childhood consisted of some form of trauma, so I had to shut down in order to survive. Which means shut down my heart. And so in arriving at a certain place in my adulthood where I felt stuck, not alive, not satisfied, I started searching out therapy, healing, better relationships, and things like that—not knowing that in doing that, one of the things that would have to happen is my heart would actually have to break open for the healing to happen so I could feel all of the past heartbreak of my childhood and not just have that peeled over and live as if it weren't a problem. And so, I think unconsciously, I picked relationships where I would be getting heartbroken so my heart would open. Because I didn't have an easy way of just opening my heart, I unconsciously had to put myself in situations where my heart would get broken open.

I built up such a very good kind of rigid structure over the trauma that I was a pretty tough nut to crack. So I think I did that unconsciously, as well as went to therapy and sought healing, not knowing it, but so I could open to all the heartbreak of the past and let it come out, and in doing that, I do understand what you're saying about reaching a place of chaos. So now that I've released a lot of the steam and felt my broken heart about my past, the chaos is kind of this feeling of, "Okay, so what I know isn't true, and I'm not sure where I'm going," so there is confusion in that time. Because there is a loss of structure.

I no longer had my old rigid structure. So I needed to create or find whatever my new softer structure would look like and how I would relate to people and relate to the world from that place. That definitely was confusing, and each time—that wasn't just a one-time thing—the more I work on myself and the further along I get in my process and my healing, the more that happens on different, deeper layers. And so there's always that process that happens; it isn't just like a one-time thing.

Healing means opening, and in the opening, you're not only going to receive healing, but you're going to be releasing any old pain or trauma that's there. And in that place, when you're releasing old pain and trauma, you're letting go of an old way of being. And so you are in a place of chaos because there's not a new way of being—quite yet.

Regarding Healing and Contemplative Being, the more and more I worked on myself through therapy and through healing, working with you, the more I spiritually healed. In clearing old trauma and taking in love, from spirit, from people, from the universe, from myself, the more I just had to clear the old trauma to be able to take in anything new. The more I have been able to hold and open to and receive love—however I take that in—the more it creates the new structure; it's not the old defensive structure, to be able to hold against what happens and just survive in the world. It leaves you feeling, "I'm just kind of surviving my life." In healing, I feel like that's always happening, but you get to a certain place after doing all of this work that the balance is kind of tipped, and instead of mostly being full of trauma and holding against it, you get to be more full of light and love, and you become bigger than the trauma, rather than the trauma feeling larger than you or all of you. So I feel like, in terms of when you're talking about the contemplative being, now I have more of a feeling of being larger than the trauma so I can work with it; it's not all of who I am, so I have more of a sense of connection to spirit, connection to love, connection to myself and other people, and I can hold any unfinished places of trauma with that love. So I feel more satisfied with life.

What Dr. Dori explains here in her story of healing is that the therapeutic process combined with a spiritual connection is what allows transformation to occur.

Full healing and transformation happen when the spiritual connection is open. Otherwise, the Ego will recycle the story over and over again. When the spiritual connection is open, then your Spirit becomes part of the healing process, and more information is contained within your Higher Self that the mind cannot access. For this reason, therapy combined with spiritual work can really accelerate the healing process.

If you are looking for something more than traditional talk therapy, then you may be seeking soul healing, spiritual healing, or energy work. There is no right or wrong. It's really what your needs are and possibly what your intuition is guiding you to. It is possible that you may need certain types of healing at certain times, and that may change over time. Keep your options open and listen to what your heart is telling you that you need.

Spiritual Healing or Energy Healing?

Soul healing, spiritual healing, and energy healing are all interchangeable terms used to describe the process of healing on the spiritual and energetic level in the body. When you want to drop down from the mind into the body and address the deeper call for healing internally, you may find energy healing hits the spot. Energy healing requires you to turn to your soul and look at what energies are stored in the body.

Transformation truly occurs when energy shifts in the body. For that to happen, it's important to understand that issues are not only in your mind; they are in your body, as well. For example, your hips hold energy, such as mothering and creativity, but also anger and stubborn resistance. Your jaw holds resentments, grudges, and unexpressed emotions. Your spine holds issues and emotions. If your back goes out, not only are you feeling physical pain, but you are feeling emotional pain, and some of it is old emotions from the past. Understanding that our issues are lodged everywhere in our being allows us to access different locations of our body to release old emotions, past issues, and stuck energy.

A healer, with intuitive abilities, is gifted in being able to tune in and guide a person through releasing and clearing the energy blocks in his or her body. Energy blocks clear when awareness, intention, and breath are directed to that area or issue. The mind will want to know how that is possible, but the soul can let go of energy blocks, and the rational mind may get in the way of that process.

Letting go of reasons and approaching your healing from the soul level is a major leap. That is spiritual healing. It means you are letting go of the mind and tuning in to the heart. It also means you are saying yes to a new way, yes to faith. As mentioned earlier, it takes courage to say *yes* to the heart.

When you say yes to the heart, you say yes to listening to your soul in communion with God. Whether your life lessons are easy or challenging, once you say yes, it's a matter of having confidence in the Divine. It's moving out of a victimizing helplessness feeling that life can knock you down to feeling the responsibility in creating the life you want. When you say yes to your heart, know that part of opening up to this calling is accepting the life lessons as well. So you might be in agreement that you will say yes and accept your life, only to find yourself faced with one of your biggest fears. Well, your higher self knows what you can take with you and what you need to overcome in order to go forward. So you are presented with this obstacle in order to heal it.

The good news is that if you say yes, then you have found trust. Yes, I accept my life. Yes, I will trust life. I will trust that I will be taken care of. Yes, I trust that I am here to participate in life in a new and truthful way. Yes, I accept the challenges and obstacles as journeys into the soul. When you say yes to your heart, you say yes to all of these. So that sense of trust creates a relaxation in knowing that no matter what, I am okay. Therefore, whatever obstacles come before me, I can handle them. They are not here to defeat me; they are here to teach me and help me grow stronger.

When I visualize saying yes to God, and the heart, life, the universe, and the calling, I visualize arms open to the sky and the heart lifted, the gaze lifted, and in pours a pillar of pure white light with rainbow light all around it. I see it come down through the crown of the head and into the heart, and it illuminates there. This visualization is a powerful one for me to hold as a representation of acceptance. What it shows is that the pathways in the energetic body have been cleared enough to let the light in. We've all heard the saying, "I can see the light." Well, not only does that imply awakening and insight to a clearer view, but it is also a sense of acceptance of the relationship with the Divine. It means you have elevated yourself to this state of awareness. You take your life as it is, and you have this perspective and watch life shift.

Imagine that you have been going through life with a negative outlook. "Nothing ever goes right for me," "I can't ever get ahead," "I'm not attractive enough, or fortunate enough," etc. Well, you've been seeing life through a particular lens that gives you one outlook on life. Now let's just say that the lens is a filter over the third eye area of your body (at your forehead), meaning the power center that governs perception and clear vision. To go a little further with this image, understand that this negative outlook was a learned behavior. Perhaps one of your parents had a similar view of life that you took on as your own. So now, let's say that one bad thing after another keeps happening to you, until you really can't take it anymore. You decide you need to get some help in getting insight into why this keeps happening. So you go to see a therapist, a healer, or a very insightful friend who helps you uncover that you have been living a victim's role in your life. Your negative outlook is perpetuating more negativity. You've been so engrained to believe this negativity that you don't even know you do it. Your options are to reject this information or to accept it and let your perception change.

Let's just say you choose to accept that you have had a negative outlook. Once you accept it, something will shift. You've brought it out of the shadow and into the light. Now, you can choose not to see life that way anymore. So you make a conscious effort to shift this outlook on life by thinking positively about yourself and others. Over time and through practice, your outlook on life really does shift. So now that the energetic blindfold over your brow is removed, there is space for more Divine Light to come in. This is a powerful shift. Things begin to turn around. You start to see more positive things happening to you in your life. You choose to accept at least one thing about yourself, and that opens a door to a different possibility. Now, the next step is to trust that if you stay with this new perspective, it won't go away. What do you do? You accept a little more.

The more you say yes, the more you clear out energetically to allow more light to come in. The soul wants to be light and connect to God. That's the ultimate goal: To connect to oneness and be in that light. Another way of saying it is that the light is the vibration of joy, love, and happiness, and that's what we aspire to. Well, the more you heal the energy blockages in the physical body, the more light you can bring in and illuminate in the physical body and radiate to the world. *The more you shine your light, the more you inspire others to do so. That is the secret to raising consciousness.*

Spiritual Healing Requires:

♥ Courage.

♥ A willingness to let go of the idea that a reason exists for wounds. There can be many layers to our wounds. If the mind gets in the way, trying to reason with the wound, we can actually block the healing process. Getting stuck on needing a reason for why things happened the way they did can actually create more frustration, and in some cases, re-traumatization. Wounds are not always reasonable. Trauma is not reasonable. That's what makes "trauma" trauma—the simple fact that it can't always be reasoned with. So do the best you can at *being* with the emotions, and the tools you will learn will support you in healing the wounds.

♥ Opening up to God, Grace, or whatever sacred term helps you feel your Divine connection.

♥ Slowing down enough to get in touch with yourself—to self-connect. How do you do this? Through meditation, contemplation, and breath—all of which strengthen intuition.

REFLECTION QUESTIONS

Theme:
How to Heal

Step 1. Talk or journal about how you moved from Chaos to Healing, or how you maneuver through chaos and take action to heal at the same time.

If sharing with another person, be concise, to the point, and acknowledge the feelings that were there at the time for you. If emotions from the past are still present for you, name them. To guide you from Chaos to clarity, consider the questions in Step 2. Also, in the next section, "Healing Guide," you will learn different tools for healing. If you are co-reading this book with others and sharing your process, your discussion may deepen after reading the healing guide. For now, discuss the following questions and experience the Guided Meditation.

Step 2. Consider the Following Questions:

- ♥ Are you pursuing healing? If so, what does it look like?
- ♥ Do you know that you can heal yourself, your life, and your situation, even if healing doesn't look like your expectations?
- ♥ What healing techniques have you tried?
- ♥ What new healing techniques are you interested in trying that you have not tried before?
- ♥ Are you tuning into yourself and listening to what you need?
- ♥ Are you letting yourself feel your feelings without making yourself wrong for having them?
- ♥ How do you stop yourself from healing on a deeper level? Describe how you sabotage yourself from healing or getting better.

♥ Describe your fully healed self and what your life looks like from feeling optimum body, mind, and spirit, wellness.

♫ **GUIDED MEDITATION AUDIO**

Log in to www.SchoolofIntuitiveStudies.com through the Expanding Your Heart link to receive your guided meditation titled "A Guided Meditation for Healing."

Chapter 7

HEALING GUIDE

"Facing your lows—your anger, loneliness, greed, fears,
depressions, and conflicts—is the most productive fire of
purification you can find.... As your connection with the spirit deepens,
you might even choose to seek out those things that
bring your attachments to the surface, so that you might
confront them and free your awareness from them....
You can no longer let them have their way.
So you ask for a hotter fire, a fiercer confrontation....
When you want to burn away the grip of your ego on
your awareness you'll endure whatever is
needed to clean up your life."

— Ram Dass

Now that you have read about healing, you may be wondering what
are some tools on how you can move through the stages of Chaos and
Healing. Below are three categories to consider when approaching
your healing process: your physical body, your mind and emotions,
and your Soul.

Healing the Body

Healing is a body, mind, and spirit process. If the physical body is not cared for, it effects how you feel, which can trigger deep, old emotions. When you are physically toxic and emotional, you don't feel good, so it's hard to access the Soul. For this reason, it is important to consider that part of your true healing and personal growth includes diet, exercise, and deep care for the body.

I am not a dietician or nutritionist, but I do recommend you explore ways to make healthy choices around food. So much information is available these days on food and nutrition, and it just takes some personal willpower to seek out information on what suits your body. In my own journey, I have sought out all different kinds of health regimens and exercise routines. I have been gluten free, dairy free, vegetarian, non-vegetarian, paleo, on the candida diet—you name it, I've probably tried it. Once I realized that part of what upsets my system around food has nothing to do with diet, but how I live in my body, everything began to change.

What helped me sort out what I should and shouldn't eat was more about relaxing my body, breathing, meditating, and letting go of stress. I have an overachiever personality, which has shot my cortisol levels through the roof, thrown my hormones off, and therefore, detrimentally affected my digestion, sleep, anxiety, and feelings about myself.

It wasn't until I immersed myself back into meditation, breathing, and yoga that my energy relaxed and I made healthy choices around food.

Yoga has been my ultimate source for balancing my body, mind, and spirit. I began my yoga practice in 1993, and since then, my yoga journey has led me through a spectrum of styles and philosophies. I recommend yoga for everyone who is looking to grow spiritually, and for overall health and wellness. Initially, you may try a class for the physical benefits of yoga. However, yoga poses are only one fraction of what yoga is. If you explore yoga's ancient roots, you will learn how breathing techniques can heal the body, how mantras and chanting can help clear blocks in your system, how to feed yourself in a balanced way, and how to open the Spiritual Heart.

This process is not quick, however. Pattabi Jois, the great teacher of Ashtanga yoga, once said, "Do your practice and all is coming." If you find yoga in your life, you will have an incredible process for healing your body, balancing your life, releasing stress, quieting the mind, and opening your heart.

One definition of yoga is *union*, which refers to union with the Divine in the physical body or to center the spirit in the body. It is possible that your yoga is walking, biking, running, strength training, swimming, or movement of other kinds. Whatever exercise you choose, as long as it brings you to your center and purifies your mind, you can consider it to be an aspect of yoga. Just notice whether your activity increases your stress or anxiety or whether it helps you feel more centered and connected to yourself. If buzzing from a lot of cardio, for example, you may benefit from a counter-balance of stretching and resting.

So when you are in Chaos, you may be inclined to lose mindfulness over what foods you eat and you may lose ground on taking care of your physical body. To move into the stage of Healing and remain there, you can explore ways to support your physical body. To begin, ask yourself these questions:

1. Do I need to move my body to move some of this energy I'm

sitting with?
2. Do I feel physically toxic, bloated, or sick?
3. Is my mind racing so much that I can't sit still or sleep through the night?
4. Am I forgetting to breathe?
5. What does my physical body need for self-care?

You can ask these questions to check in with yourself when you are in the stages of Chaos and Healing. Both Chaos and Healing can be very un-grounding times. Tending to your physical body is a way to ground yourself. As you tend to your physical body, you may experience emotional clearing and release. If, however, you feel okay in your physical body and are ready to address your healing on the emotional level, you may find the information in the next chapter, Contemplative Being, beneficial.

Healing Your Mind and Emotions

The mind is generally associated with thoughts and reason. Yet, for many people, thoughts stem from emotions, feelings, and belief systems. When in the stage of Healing, it is important to address underlying emotions and beliefs you were raised with that are affecting your life. For example, if you believe everyone else can succeed in life, but you can't, then your thoughts and feelings about yourself are going to organize themselves around that belief.

Where are beliefs and emotions stored in your body? They're all in your head, right? Well, a percentage of them are. The rest are in your body's energy system. Within your physical body is an energetic anatomy. The energetic anatomy is comprised of meridians, power centers (chakras), and pressure points. Emotions and beliefs exist in various areas of the energetic anatomy. In my book *Energy Healing Through the Chakras*, I talk about the energetic body, how belief systems live in various chakras in the body, and how to clear them. You can refer to this book for a deeper look at belief systems that store in the energetic body.

In the stage of Healing, you may find that what is causing you pain is not what someone did to you or what you did. What's causing you pain are your emotions, expectations, beliefs, and ultimately, your ego. The main emotions coming up for you after an Initial Heart Opening and in the stage of Chaos may have origins from early in life. One way you can address your healing process is simply by addressing how an emotion influences your life. For example, how does fear run the choices you make in life? How early on were fearful beliefs presented to you? What made you afraid? Addressing fear and its impact on your life can actually relieve all the actions and reactions you have previously made that you may be regretting.

Below are explanations of some primary emotions from an energetic and spiritual perspective and how to work with healing the energy of those emotions.

Fear

Some forms Fear may take:
- ♥ Lack
- ♥ Abandonment
- ♥ Not feeling safe
- ♥ Gluttony/hoarding
- ♥ Fear of being alone
- ♥ Fear of succeeding (solar plexus)
- ♥ Fear of being seen (solar plexus)
- ♥ Lack of trust

♥ Defensiveness
♥ Being overly-protective

Fear may be felt in a few areas of the body. For the purpose of addressing fear's deeper energetic roots, let's consider two primary areas of the body: The First Chakra (tailbone) and the Third Chakra (solar plexus). Here is how fear activates in these two areas of the body:

The First Chakra: The First Chakra represents trust in the earth element. The earth element is about grounding; connecting to family, community, food, safety, abundance; and trusting that the earth will support you. It also carries beliefs about belonging in your body and on this earth. When we have been instilled with safety and trust, we have a spiritual confidence within to trust life. When fear has been a feeling in the "air" in childhood, it becomes part of the hard-wired operating system. That means you may operate from fear without even knowing it because it was such a normal way of being. It was also normal to feel it in your family bonding, and because we recreate what is normal to us, naturally it would be brought into any other intimate relationships and connections you may have later in life.

It is important to remember that we are human, so by default, we will have fear just like any other emotion. Fear does protect us from danger, which I will explain further in the Third Chakra section. One of the primary ways fear gets introduced into our system is not even one of which we're consciously aware because it occurs on a deep subconscious level. This primary fear is created at birth through the separation from Source (God, the light, insert your own word here) into human existence.

Our spirits are free when we are in the light. When our spirit leaves the vast expansiveness and comes into a human form, fear forms. Fear then shows up as a vulnerability. We are vulnerable as babies, and therefore, we have needs. When these basic needs are not met, or they are met in an abusive way, then feelings of neglect, fear, lack of trust, etc. can form.

Some people have a very loving and nurturing childhood, but they still live with a "fear of being alone," for example. This can come from a primary fear of separation. If fear of being alone resonates for you, notice all the ways you have structured your life so you are not alone. Codependency can form to prevent that primary fear of being alone and separate. Within this chapter, I will explain ways to work with the fear, but it may be helpful to name some ways that fear of separation may affect how you operate in life and with others.

Another subconscious fear that resides within the First Chakra is the fear of death. If you narrow down your fears to one primary fear, it may be fear of dying. For example, consider these beliefs and feelings: "I don't feel safe," "I'm afraid I might fail," or "There is never enough money, love, etc." If you ask yourself, "Why?" to each of those beliefs, you will realize you have a basic fear of impermeability or death. Panic can occur when we reach a place that feels as if we may die if we speak our truth. That place, physically, is part of the body that is not living or may feel paralyzed because breath is not moving through the body when we reach deep triggering fear. One of the reasons why we are taught to breathe through panic, fear, and difficulty is because it is bringing life force into a triggered moment when the body is absent of breath and life. Consciously, you may know you are not dying, but the body is so full of fear that the breath stops and so does the flow of life.

Breathing through emotions is crucial because you are breathing fresh life into where your body is holding onto an old emotion.

The Third Chakra: The Third Chakra is the power center through which we navigate through life instinctually; we take action from it according to our innate wisdom and intuition. It is also the power center for confidence in Self and in the Divine. If we are not confident spiritually (do not have faith), some of our insecurities will show up in our human characteristics. That sense of non-security or lack of confidence lends itself to the fear of manifesting your true Self into the world. Instead, what will happen is that the Wounded Ego will take over. Self-critical and fear-based feelings and thoughts will ensue. Fear of succeeding, fear of taking action, fear of trusting yourself, and fear of choosing love are all fears that dwell within the solar plexus as a result of not being spiritually confident.

Furthermore, a direct relationship exists between being ungrounded and the solar plexus being in balance. Grounding is the downward direction of life force energy. Think of it as gravity; naturally, our grounding energy should be moving downward, in order for us to feel balanced and calm in our being. However, if fear exists in the root chakra about life or a situation, then the energy in the root reverses and goes up or goes out. The solar plexus reacts to this reversal of energy by opening up significantly. It actually blows open the Third Chakra, and it becomes too big to cord and ground into something for stability. So now, the Third Chakra power is looking for connections to feel safe. Our power (in the form of cords) reaches into other people or other situations in order to feel safe. This is a vulnerability, however, because we can't always count on others to meet our deeper need for safety and security. Others are not our spiritual source, although we may be dependent on them for that.

To heal fear in this area, it's important to ground the First Chakra energy downward, and allow the Third Chakra to relax back into who you are. When you relax back, you can connect to the feeling of the Divine hand at your back, giving you all the love and spiritual sourcing your soul needs to feel met on a soul-level. Building this connection through visualization can help establish spiritual confidence, which will allow you to center within yourself, your choices, and your relationships.

How to Work with Fear in Your Life

You can address fear in your life in many different ways. Below are steps or guidelines for an energetic approach to healing, clearing, or quelling fear:

Step 1. Reflect

First, reflect on the patterns of how you act or react from fear. Remember that fear is a natural emotion, and to strive to remove fear completely from your body may not be realistic. To learn how to manage fear when it comes up may be a more realistic goal. Start to look at life decisions and actions you make out of fear. In the stage of Healing, you want to be really honest with yourself and take responsibility for what led you to this point. It's not someone else's fault. It is your responsibility to be centered and conscious enough to make clear choices in life. Forgive yourself for any actions you have made from not being aware at the time. You did the best you could at the time to handle that life situation. The statements below can help you identify where fear shows up in your life.

- ♥ I push people away to protect myself from feeling vulnerable
- ♥ I put my problems on other people
- ♥ I am afraid to do something alone or for myself
- ♥ I would never do that (referring to something positive, but bold)
- ♥ I isolate myself

♥ I smother myself with other people so I don't have to deal with parts of me I don't like
♥ I can't succeed
♥ I am stuck
♥ I am afraid of love—to feel love or to tell someone I love him/her
♥ I am not a hugger or affectionate
♥ I am afraid of the unknown
♥ When I can't control the future or a situation, I feel anxious, angry, and out of control

Feel free to contemplate what additional fears arise for you.

Step 2. Locate the Feeling of Fear in the Body and Breathe

Direct your focus to an area of the body where you notice fear lives. We breathe automatically to live, but when we direct breath with intention to various areas of the body, it becomes a tool for healing. Direct your breath to the area of the body where the emotion is stored, and breathe into it. Think about the systems in your body, organs, or even cells; think about limbs, skin, etc. Breathe into the fear. Breathe into any images, thoughts, or words that arise and are attached to that fear as you are breathing. Don't judge them or yourself; just keep breathing through the fear.

Step 3. Visualize

Visualizations may help you in clearing the fear. You can try to visualize or create a "feels like/looks like/smells like" metaphor for your emotion. Answer questions like: What does it look like? What is the consistency? What color does it have? You might get responses like: fire, smoky clouds, quicksand, sticky glue, etc. To clear, think of how you would deal with whatever appeared to you. For instance: How would you put out fire? Think about what visuals you would create to clear/transform that image and the emotion you associate with it.

If the fear feels so big that you are disconnecting, getting sleepy, or feeling distracted, then call in the image of white light or an angel to surround you to create comfort. Possibly, whenever the fear originated, it was a very unsafe situation so you may need to recreate the feeling of comfort and safety to relax your system and let the fear clear more thoroughly.

Step 4. Interview the Fear

Sometimes, it is valuable to find out the history of the fear and where it came from. Sometimes, it is not necessary because trying to figure out *why* gets the mind in the way of the soul letting go. If exploring the fear's origins feels important to you, consider this step:
Talk to the fear with the intention of getting to know it better. You are a journalist, and your fear is an interviewee. Ask questions such as: Where did this fear come from? Did it come from you or someone else? How old is it? Do you need it anymore? Is it ready to go? If so, take some deep breaths and let it release down a long beam of light from you to the center of the earth. In the center of the earth, imagine that the fear dissolves into the core and transforms into clear love.

Step 5. Let Go

You are surely familiar with the term "let go": *let go of the past; let go of how you feel right now and move on.* Learning to let go on an energetic level is extremely important and helps you move forward in your life, especially when the mind can't let go. But *how* do you let go? Letting go on an energetic level starts with creating an exit or outlet for energy to move through.

Here are outlets through which you can move energy by means of focused breath work:

1. **The Grounding Cord:** It runs from your hips to the center of the earth.
2. **The Crown of your head:** You can open up a pillar or pipeline to the cosmos and let the energy release through the top of your head.
3. **Bubble of Light:** Create a bubble out in front of you, place the energy in the bubble, and send the bubble far away from you.
4. **Expel out of your body in all directions:** Just breathe and exhale the energy out of your system, through the front and back side. This works especially well with anger.
5. **Use your voice:** You may need to say something, yell something, or speak to someone in order to let the energy go.

Step 6. Reprogram

What is the opposite of fear for you? Your answer may be different from someone else's answer. What comes to you is exactly what you need to fill that space that was created from the fear releasing. In energy work, you *always* want to replace something negative that you've released with a positive feeling, image, or word. Otherwise, the space where the negativity existed is unclaimed and negativity can fill right back in there. So declare what intention you would like to live from, and breathe it into that space. It can be a new belief, such as "I am love" or "I am powerful." It could even be the feeling of presence and empowerment. It could also be a color or an image that depicts how you want to live in your body. Additionally, there could be a quote, song, poem, or some other wording that would speak to the POWER of your spirit and how you overcame the fear. These words might also mirror what you want when you think of what your life will be like on the other side of fear.

Step 7. Take Action

The fear you just released has been there a long time, so it will take some conscious effort on your part to live from your new intention. What actions will you take to live from your new belief, new feeling, or from this shifted place? Take out a piece of paper and list your action steps. Do it now and follow through by taking those steps.

When moving through the first Three Stages of the Spiritual Opening, you may be finding out that you made some major mistakes because you were choosing fear over faith or love. Go easy on yourself. Accept responsibility where it is yours to accept, and choose to transform that fear. Make a change. You have an entire lifetime and will learn many lessons. You will also have many opportunities to overcome. In the next section, we will cover healing that can occur through Guilt and Shame.

Facing Fear

Saying yes to the heart can happen when you are ready for it. In fact, it may be long overdue. It might bring up fear even to think about it, but think about how many times you let fear stop you. You didn't go for something you wanted because you didn't want to hurt someone's feelings, or you were afraid to speak your true feelings, so you stuffed them inside. People often self-sabotage because of fear.

You have to be willing to walk into the fear. Why? Because when you face fear and stand still breathing through the most fearful moments, that's when you overcome it. That's when you no longer fear the fear itself because you are choosing to be awake amid the fear. When that happens, change comes. Possibilities are endless because the universe knows you're not afraid to receive. The fear dissolves. There's no fear to block it, and even if there is some, you know how to stand in it and take care of yourself in moments when the fear comes up.

Breathing and carrying life-force energy into your body when the fear triggers will tell your body you are alive. You will obtain stamina because your body will remember that the next time you are afraid, you will return to that exact same feeling of breath and life force moving through your body. If you've ever taken a yoga class and held a challenging pose with deep breathing, released into a counterpose, and then returned to the challenging pose, and you were able to go beyond your peak point, then this is the same idea. Your body remembers where to return to if you stay awake and conscious that you will breathe in the moment of fear, or whatever emotion is present.

Fear can be a warning signal against danger, and it can help you discern what is safe for you and what isn't. However, we can grow a great deal by conquering our fears. I do know that, consciously or unconsciously, when there is an experience where I feel fear arise, I walk into the center of it. I gravitate toward it, and I try to conquer it with presence, breath, and trust. Do I overcome it? Yes. The fear dissipates. Does it come back? Sometimes, but lessened. So I try to conquer it again. It reminds me of the days when I first started to perform as a singer/songwriter. Here I was pouring my heart and soul out in song and putting myself up on a stage in front of people for pure evaluation of whether I was good or not. I was terrified, and I often felt traumatized when I came off stage, but I kept doing it. Over time, the fear dissolved, and I was able to shine with the songs.

So what does it mean to conquer fear? It means that you are in trust with your connection to the Divine and you feel that sense in your body that "I am connected to the truth of my being and I am okay." Many people worry about whether or not their son or daughter is going to be okay, or their loved ones are going to be okay. When you have those worries, they reflect your own personal lack of trust in believing you are okay. Instead, you choose to live with fear. The Divine plan for all beings is to commune with God and value human existence. If we choose to do that, we have a greater sense of purpose and connection. If we do not choose it, then we grow more fearful of our fate. We have resisted the life-force energy that could actually support our path and wellbeing.

Guilt and Shame

Some forms Guilt and Shame may take:

- ♥ Codependency
- ♥ Low self-esteem
- ♥ Fearing confrontation (Feeling bad about confronting)
- ♥ Trouble asking for what you want
- ♥ Manipulating to get needs met
- ♥ Intimacy issues

Keep in mind that the Ego is the part of our being that keeps us emotionally attached to the material world. Although, we do need the Ego in order to manifest ourselves into the world, we also have to be aware of the wounds the Ego carries and reminds us of (sometimes daily). In other words, the Ego's wounds will make up our conscious and subconscious thoughts.

Just like fear, shame and guilt are part of the Ego consciousness. You are not shame. You are not guilt. Rather, attachments to something in the past (or sometimes the future) will bring these emotions to the surface. They may even underlay patterns and conditioning, where you don't even realize you're making choices out of guilt or shame.

In this section, we will address how guilt and shame affect you on an emotional, spiritual, and energetic level. We will also address ways of providing healing around guilt and shame.

Differentiating Between Guilt and Shame

Guilt is when you feel "bad" because you did something wrong. It's possible that you were told to do something and didn't follow through with it, and then you feel guilty for not obeying the request. Guilt can be a corrective emotion, showing you that you would like to behave in a different way around an experience. In this way, guilt can be helpful. It directs you toward living in more integrity. Healthy guilt is self-generated: "I wish I hadn't done that."

Shame happens when you get the sense that who you are is bad. This belief can form when you did not originally have a sense that what you were doing was bad, so the mistake was not initially self-generated. It may come from your family, group of friends, or society in a way that allows you the feeling of being accepted into a tribe or community. If you go against the "tribal belief," then you feel that "who I am is bad." To belong, especially as children, we accept the tribal belief because we need others in order to survive. Over time, the tribal belief becomes your belief, and so does the feeling of shame, should you go against that belief.

Shame is our fear that we are not good enough to belong, that we are not good enough to experience love and inclusion in those groups to which we wish to belong. Shame is a conflict between our inner self (higher self, if you will) who knows us and where we want to go, and our ego self, who wants to do what is expected to belong, in order to ensure the safety of our physical self.

To put this differentiation simply: Guilt is when you feel you did something wrong. Shame is when you feel that *who you are* is wrong. In the stage of Healing, it may be natural to consider the ways that guilt and shame have had impact on the choices you've made in your life and on your upbringing.

The Effects of Guilt and Shame on the Body

Guilt and shame can be very gripping feelings in the body. No matter what your intuition is telling you, you will *never* listen to it if guilt or shame is in place. They are very strong feelings if they are given priority. Both of these emotions are of an extremely low vibration, and they will pull your spirit down.

Check in with yourself on where you feel guilt and shame in your own body. Is it in your heart? Your gut? Your throat? You may feel it in various places when you are triggered. Every person's experience will be different, but below is some advice on where guilt and shame could reside in your body; it will be helpful information if you are looking to address your shame and guilt from an energy healing perspective.

Guilt about something in the past may be felt higher up in the body and often in the heart. Why? Because honesty keeps you in right alignment with Source. If you do something that is out of alignment, then you may feel twisted inside; that is one way guilt is felt. The heart often is the place of consciousness in the body that will react if you have knowingly done something out of alignment.

In the Third Chakra (solar plexus), you may also feel some body-sensations. Your body may not be able to digest something that feels out of integrity. So you may feel sick to your stomach until action is taken to correct the feeling. On the other hand, if you were "guilt tripped" early on in life, then the programming for the early onset of these two emotions may be lower in the body. The Third Chakra may be where you internalize that guilt until you find a way to "right the wrong."

Shame, on the other hand, is a deep insult to energy in the lower half of the body. It often is something instilled by deep beliefs in an attempt to align a spirit to a dogma (spiritual or cultural). It is a way of instilling morals and beliefs. As a spiritually progressing soul and through energy healing, you can bring truth and Spiritual Consciousness to your choice of whether these beliefs are ones that work for you, or whether they need to be amended. Guilt tripping or shaming you may have been a way to control you, but again, as you take responsibility for how you want to live *your* life, you get to choose what beliefs you want to live from and what beliefs no longer serve you.

When you get to the stage of Healing, you are shifting your bonding. Bonding originates in your family, and it includes what you believe in order to be accepted in the "tribe." Shifting your bonding means you are finding healthier ways of being yourself with others. It doesn't always mean you cut off your family or people, but you learn to choose yourself and love yourself in a way that shifts the dynamic or how much you take on that does not belong to you.

On the other hand, that may mean choosing new friends, creating boundaries, and surrounding yourself with people you can bond with on the new beliefs you are choosing to live from. Being able to recognize shame and guilt as emotions in your system will help you have enough separation to make choices you didn't know you had in your family bonding.

For example, let's say, hypothetically speaking, I was someone who lived with the bonding that it was my responsibility to be quiet, a good girl, and not express my feelings because one of my parents couldn't handle emotions. So every time I had an emotion, I was punished (shamed) for having feelings. Then I felt guilty if I did anything that would rock the boat and make my parent upset. I learned that it wasn't okay for me to feel my feelings, and if I did feel anything, I certainly wouldn't go to my parent, so I'm wounded now around trusting that anyone will hear or receive me. Now, let's say I go through therapy or somewhere else in my life I learn that it wasn't okay for me not to be able to have my feelings. That throws a wrench in every way that I act or interact with people. My dynamic with people was that I became a pleaser, a placater, and I believed it was my responsibility to fix everyone else's feelings. So if I was not supposed to be that person, then who am I? You mean I matter? I have a choice and I'm allowed to have feelings?

The impact of shame and guilt can shape a person's entire way of being in the world. Once you start to heal the emotional and psychological impact of shame and guilt (which can be done in therapy or through a healing practitioner), your Soul can then make choices about how you want to live in yourself from a place of self-love. That may mean choosing new friends, changing your habits, making healthier choices, crying if you're sad, or being angry if you're angry!

How to Heal around Guilt and Shame

When you are moving through clearing Guilt and Shame, consider breathing into *anywhere* you feel them in your body. The suggested locations above are guidelines, but trust your intuition about where guilt/shame (if at all) are felt in your system.

Please note that anger may come up with shame or guilt, and it is important to feel it. In the next section, you will read about how to work with anger so you will have further opportunity to purge if necessary.

Step 1. Getting Real

Forget about trying to clear every single emotion in your body down to having no emotions. It won't be possible. You are human, you will have feelings, and the Divine loves you as you are, feelings and all. So, instead, just focus on letting go of some old baggage, stuck feelings from the past, and what pains you. This guide is meant to help you move through the stages of your heart and soul expanding. The question I like to ask myself is "What will help me feel more free around this situation?" If the answer I receive is to feel my anger, then I feel the anger to that triggered memory as much as I can until I'm ready not to toxify myself with my own anger anymore, so I can forgive. Will anger come for me again with another memory? Sure, why not? So I'll give myself permission to feel exactly how I feel then, too. I will not shame myself for being real. That is my recommendation for you.

Step 2. Reflect and Gain Perspective

Just as you would with Fear, reflect on how Shame affects your actions and reactions in your life. Are there any beliefs you adopted in order to have a bond to your family or friends. Is there a deep feeling of embarrassment? Do you feel guilty about something you did that needs to be corrected? Start tuning into the word "shame" or "guilt" and see what comes up for you. Then, start to look at decisions and actions you make out of guilt and shame. Just as with fear, in the stage of Healing, you want to be really honest with yourself and take responsibility for what led you to this point. Instead of blaming a parent or

170

someone whom you feel may have shamed or guilt-tripped you, have your feelings about it. Feel your true feelings. Then look at it from the perspective that *you* adopted that shame or guilt because you wanted to be loved and accepted. You may have felt then that you didn't have a choice. However, now you do. *You* decide not to take on the guilt or shame any longer. Remember: As a spiritually progressing soul, you get to choose how you want to *be* in your life. Forgive yourself for any actions you previously took from just wanting love and acceptance. You did the best you could do at the time to handle life then.

Step 3. Locate the Feelings of Guilt and Shame in the Body and Breathe

Direct your breath and focus to an area of the body where you feel shame or guilt. You may feel it anywhere in the body. However, I suggest focusing on the Second Chakra area, which is in the pelvis. The reason is that this power center is about owning your emotional center, your sensitivity, and your creativity. It is also the power center for sexuality and relationships. In this power center, we carry information on how well we center ourselves and feel our true feelings within all our relationships, especially our primary ones. Guilt and shame affect the Second Chakra area because when they are internalized, they cause you to believe you can't own your center or have your feelings in the body's power center. Therefore, you surrender your needs for the other person. When guilt and shame are affected in this area, it affects creativity, sensuality, sexuality, and being in your sweetness. It also creates a very judgmental critical voice because this part of your being is mirroring the parenting you received. Many people do not necessarily feel the emotional impact on the pelvis or tailbone areas, but these two power centers, the First and Second Chakras, carry primary programming on how we subconsciously operate in the world. So, my suggestion is to direct your breath to the pelvis to release any guilt or shame held there from way back in time.

Just as mentioned in the fear section, direct your breath to the area of the body where the emotion is stored and breathe into it. Think about the pelvis and any other systems in your body, organs, or even cells; think about limbs, skin, etc. Breathe into guilt and shame. Breathe into any images, thoughts, or words that arise and are attached to those emotions as you are breathing. Don't judge them or yourself; just keep breathing through the feelings.

Step 4. Let Go

As mentioned in the fear section, you are surely familiar with the term "let go": *let go of the past; let go of how you feel right now, and move on*. Learning to let go on an energetic level is extremely important and helps you move forward in your life, especially when the mind can't let go. But *how* do you let go? Letting go on an energetic level starts with creating an exit, or outlet, for energy to move through.

Here are outlets through which you can move energy by means of focused breath work:

1. **The Grounding Cord:** It runs from your hips to the center of the earth.
2. **The Crown of your head:** You can open up a pillar or pipeline to the cosmos and let the energy release through the top of your head.
3. **Bubble of Light:** Create a bubble out in front of you. Place the energy in the bubble and send the bubble far away from you.
4. **Expel out of your body in all directions:** Just breathe and ex-hale the energy out of your system, through the front and back side. This works especially well with anger.

5. **Use your voice:** You may need to say something, yell something, or speak to someone in order to let the energy go.

Step 5. Connect to your Genuine Goodness

While clearing guilt and shame, know that your true nature is to be *good*. As mentioned earlier, guilt and shame leave the imprint that you are bad or you did something bad. However, especially in childhood, the true spirit of genuine goodness is very natural. Is it possible that whatever shame you took on was because you wanted to do the right thing, and that was the right thing at the time? Is it possible you feel guilty because there is a part of goodness inside you that wants to correct the past? You were operating from the genuine goodness inside you, and that goodness is still there to help you make any corrections your soul needs to ease the pain of guilt and shame.

Step 6. Forgiveness

Forgiveness takes you out of prison with the past. It doesn't mean the other person gets away with whatever actions hurt you. It means you are no longer willing to let the hurt keep you stuck in the past. Forgiveness helps you free up your energy, detoxify your memory bank of painful memories, allow more freedom into your life, and move on. In order to forgive fully, you have to feel completely released from the anger, guilt, or shame feeling. Forgiveness is taking yourself out of karmic prison with the other person and agreeing that you are no longer holding him or her responsible for your feelings. Forgive yourself, forgive others, and ask the Divine for forgiveness, too, if necessary. If forgiveness is not possible right now, go back to Steps 2 and 3. You won't be able to forgive if you're still angry or hurt. Give yourself the gift of having full permission to feel your feelings about the situation. It may take some time to feel everything. Hand over to the Divine what you cannot handle and ask for help. If you cannot yet forgive the other person, forgive yourself for anything your system is not letting go. Forgiveness is a spiritual act of inviting the Divine to help you in this human experience of suffering.

Step 7. Visualize Yourself as Centered

What does it look like or feel like to be in your center? Because guilt and shame feel like such a deep feeling in the center of the heart, core, or Second Chakra, I like to visualize the presence of my light illuminating from the center of my being. Remember: When healing guilt and shame, you are making a choice to live from owning your true feelings in your body. How do you imagine that would look in how you carry yourself in the world? How would you radiate owning your center? However that looks to you, visualize it and be it.

Step 8. Reprogram

What is the opposite of guilt or shame for you? Your answer may be different from someone else's. What comes to you is exactly what you need to fill the space created from the fear releasing. In energy work, when you release something negative, you *always* want to fill that space with a positive feeling, image, or word. Otherwise, the space is unclaimed and negativity can fill right back in there. So declare what intention you would like to live from, and breathe it into that space. It can be a new belief, such as "I can have my feelings," or "I am true." It could be the feeling of confidence and self-love. It could also be a color or an image that depicts how you want to live in your body. Additionally, it could be a quote, song, poem, or other wording that would speak to the *power* of your spirit and how you healed the wound of shame and guilt. These words might also mirror what you want when you think of what your life will be like on the other side of shame or guilt.

Step 9. Take Action

Shame and guilt may have shaped how you felt about yourself for a long time. They may have even shaped decisions you have made in life. So it will take some conscious effort on your part to live from your new intention and choose yourself. What actions will you take to live from your new belief, new feeling, or from this shifted place? Take out a piece of paper and list your action steps. Complete this step now.

Take some deep breaths now. While going through this Healing Guide section, it may be difficult to work through these emotions, but hang in there. Exploring and processing these feelings is necessary to make way for your light. Take the time you need to process. Talk to others if necessary, but stay committed to working through the feelings. There are a few more emotions to cover, so keep going.

Anger

How do you know whether you live with unprocessed anger? Believe it or not, you may be living with the feeling of unprocessed anger without ever realizing it. Here are some signs:

- ♥ Being *reactionary*
- ♥ Expecting others to know what you need rather than asking for what you need
- ♥ Avoidance behavior
- ♥ Being judgmental
- ♥ Holding grudges or contempt
- ♥ Weight issues
- ♥ Being accusatory; blaming others; using indirect speech (typically being rude/snide); passive aggressive behavior
- ♥ Engaging in "punishing" behavior, to self and others

♥ Shutting down unconsciously or to avoid feeling
♥ Blaming

Anger can be a difficult emotion to own because in the U.S. and other cultures, we're not always taught how to express anger appropriately or in healthy ways. Instead, we may have been punished for expressing anger as a child. That taught us that having anger is bad instead of teaching us that anger is a normal feeling, and there are ways to cope with anger. Being punished for being angry or not being validated for having feelings will eventually develop into rage. So many of us have suppressed anger because of how we were taught that to heal angry reactions in life requires us to heal the suppressed anger within us.

Anger typically shows up consciously during a serious threat of physical danger or when someone crosses one of our boundaries. Most of the time, we are consciously able to recall what made us angry. Not being able to remember our anger's source is a likely indicator of unprocessed anger. Unprocessed anger is exactly what it says it is: anger that was suppressed so left unprocessed. For instance, you feel angry and hurt by how you are being treated (perhaps when you were a child by an adult, or even yesterday by a coworker); you feel angry and hurt, but for a variety of reasons, you can't express your anger, so you suppress it; you stuff it away.

Anger can also be present in subconscious ways. For example, when the body experiences trauma, suppressed anger may surface later. Suppressed anger expresses itself typically through symptoms in the body: weight gain, a sore throat, anxiety, digestive issues, ulcers, liver issues, hives, eczema, etc.

Anger can be a way of saying, "I feel hurt." If we can't express our hurts, we get angry. If no one listens to us, or we feel abandoned, rejected, neglected, etc., we feel hurt. As children we may not always have the words to say, "You hurt me." Instead, we get angry.

Being neglected, not getting needs met, not getting heartfelt attention, or being a child of substance abuse, alcoholism, or narcissism are all sources of childhood anger—and potentially suppressed anger.

Anger *can* be useful, too. If you have been repressed or fighting an uphill battle for too long in your life, you may begin to feel fed up. The feeling of "Enough!" may actually be anger surfacing for the purpose of helping you initiate change in a potentially unpleasant situation such as a soul-killing job or unhealthy relationship. In these situations, anger can be useful in propelling change to happen.

Anger can be felt in various places in the body. For healing purposes, it's important to breathe through wherever you are feeling the anger. Generally, anger is a full-body feeling and propels movement. Because it is a *big* emotion, anger needs expansive, active expression. It requires expelling energy through big body movements and through breath work.

How to Work with Healing Old Anger:

You can work with addressing anger in your life in many different ways. Below are guidelines on an energetic approach to healing, clearing, or quelling anger:

Step 1. Reflect

First reflect on the patterns of how you act or react from anger. As with prior emotions discussed, anger is a natural emotion so to strive to remove it completely from your body may not be realistic. However, you can release bottled up anger and learn how to manage it when it comes up. Start to look at yourself, your body, the ways you are with people, and life decisions and actions you make out of anger. In the stage of Healing, you want to be really honest with yourself and take responsibility for what led you to this point. Was anger a part of what propelled an Initial Heart Opening? If so, that anger probably needed to happen so you would see you had anger that needed to be addressed. Let go of blaming others and be willing to take responsibility for the anger inside you. Consider whether any of the following statements are true for you:

♥ I act in defensive ways
♥ I yell a lot and put my feelings on other people
♥ I control with anger
♥ I cross boundaries by yelling, screaming, and not listening
♥ I'm not happy with my life
♥ I blame others for my situation
♥ I choose to ignore what I don't want to deal with
♥ I'm openly critical of others
♥ I'm really nice, but deep down, I complain or am critical
♥ I judge people
♥ I act out with anger when I am hurt

Feel free to contemplate what additional statements come up for you.

Step 2. Locate the Feeling of Anger in the Body and Breathe

Direct your focus to an area where you feel anger in your body. We breathe automatically to live, but when we direct breath with intention to various areas of the body, it becomes a tool for healing. Direct your breath to the area of the body where the emotion is stored, and breathe into it. Think about the systems in your body, organs, or even cells; think about limbs, skin, etc. Breathe into the anger. Breathe into any images, thoughts, or words that arise and are attached to that fear as you are breathing. Don't judge it or yourself; just keep breathing through the anger.

Step 3. Move Your Body

As mentioned earlier, anger needs to move out of the body. Give yourself time and space to move your body physically so you can move the anger energetically. Any activity such as shaking your arm, kicking actions with your legs, walking, running, or even verbally expressing what is bottled up releases the energy from your throat. Crying can even be an anger release. Your body wants to purge the energy outward, so don't hold it in; let it out.

Step 3. Visualize

Sometimes, it can be helpful to visualize a child-age version of yourself in a room or a moment in your past and allow that child to express his or her anger. For example, if you are angry about something from when you were ten years old, then visualize your ten-year-old self in a room having a tantrum. It's possible that your ten-year-old self did not get to express anger at that time and still needs to. This exercise is *wonderful* for clearing past, bottled-up feelings. If you allow yourself to visualize your past ages as expressing their feelings, you are clearing stuck energy!

If anger feels so big that you are shutting down or disassociating, then call in the image of white light or an angel to surround you and create comfort. Just as with fear, it is possible that whenever the anger originated, it was a very unsafe situation, so you may need to recreate the feeling of comfort and safety to give your system permission to feel what is true.

179

Step 4. Interview the Anger

It may be helpful to interview your anger to explore its source, but this process is not always helpful while you are angry. Just with any emotional releasing, if the mind tries to figure it out, the mind may get carried away in the story and justifications. Instead, just feel the feelings. Once you have given yourself room to feel the anger, you may get to its source. Generally, as mentioned earlier, the anger results from being hurt, so when you dig deep, you may hit grief.

Once you have completed Step 4 and understand what's beneath the anger, you may feel you are in a more grounded place. Then you can ask such questions as: Where did this feeling come from? Did it come from me or someone else? How old is it? Do I need it anymore? Is it ready to go? If so, take some deep breaths and let it release down a long beam of light from you to the center of the earth. In the center of the earth, imagine the fear dissolving into the core and transforming into clear love.

Step 5. Let Go and Forgive

Let go emotionally and energetically, and forgive those who have hurt you. This is your ticket to spiritual freedom. Healing old anger is like taking yourself out of stewing in your own pasta for way too long. Release your anger, move your body, and forgive yourself and all beings for their actions created from their suffering or unawareness.

Step 6. Reprogram

What is the opposite of anger for you? Love? Peace? Acceptance? Without even thinking too much about it, what's the first answer that comes? What comes to you is exactly what you need to fill that space that was created from the fear releasing. In energy work, you *always* want to fill a space where you released something negative with a positive feeling, image, or word. Otherwise, the space is unclaimed and negativity can fill right back in there. So declare what intention you would like to live from, and breathe it into that space. It can be a new belief, such as "I am peace" or "I am free." It could even be the feeling of presence and empowerment. It could also be a color or an image that depicts how you want to live in your body. Additionally, there could be a quote, song, poem, or other wording that would speak to the *power* of your spirit and how you overcame the fear. These words might also mirror what you want when you think of what your life will be like on the other side of fear.

Step 7. Take Action

What action steps are you willing to take to step more fully into the power of love, acceptance, peace, or whatever your intention is for yourself? It will take some conscious effort on your part to live from your new intention. Take out a piece of paper and list what actions you will take to live from your new intention or belief so you can feel shifted. Do it now and follow through.

Go easy on yourself around healing anger in your system. You may have become very used to the anger, and being without it could bring up an odd feeling of loneliness because you miss the feeling. Remember to fill the space in your being with love for yourself. You are healing. It takes great courage to heal. One more layer of emotion remains to look at, and it's often the emotion that opens the heart. Keep going on to the next section on healing grief.

Grief

Some forms Grief may take:

♥   Sadness, and its deeper version: sorrow
♥   Denial/Avoidance
♥   Depression
♥   A protective heart
♥   Isolation/pushing people away, even with kindness
♥   Feeling stuck or at a crossroads in life
♥   Fear of commitment and/or intimacy
♥   Rejecting others before being rejected yourself

While grief is a form of sadness, it is also the doorway to a major spiritual opening in the Heart Chakra. The Heart has three layers, or levels, that are interdependent and related: the Physical Heart, the Emotional Heart, and the Spiritual Heart. The heart's physical health can be impacted by the state of both the emotional and spiritual heart. The spiritual heart holds the soul's deepest mission while you are here on earth. Ultimately, that includes being an expression of pure love, including sharing love and receiving love. When, however, the emotions of the heart are not processed or worked through, the emotional heart can keep us from evolving to a spiritual state of being.

Grief in the Body

Grief is the primary emotion held in the heart, but it can reside in other places in the body, too, and the heart can also contain other emotions other than grief. Grief can result from such things as: loss, divorce, death of a loved one, not getting to live your full self, or not receiving the kind of love you needed when you needed it. It is so important that grief be felt at the time of the original impact or hurt. If it is not felt, it gets suppressed, after which protection mechanisms form in order to prevent future harm from occurring.

The paradox of protection mechanisms is that they not only protect from potential future harm, but they create a barrier that makes it difficult to feel and receive deep love going forward. Needless to say, this dynamic does not help you evolve past the feelings of hurt and pain. Protection mechanisms are there to keep intense feelings at bay. They can show up as numbing feelings or feeling shut down. You may not consciously be afraid to feel the sadness of loss, but somewhere in your subconscious is an operating system at work that says the grief is too big to feel so I will shut it down.

It's important to feel and process grief so it doesn't feed your fears or block your intuition and clarity of purpose. When grief is present, it may be challenging to feel your intuition. It's like foggy emotional clouds over the heart, but once they clear, your shining intuitive light will come through.

How to Work With Grief

Step 1. Breathe

Breath circulates through the heart and lungs. Grief sits in the heart and lungs. When you engage in conscious breath aimed at processing grief, you are literally flushing out your lungs to rid them of grief and pain.

Step 2. Feel

Feel the pain, the hurt, the anger, and the sadness. Feel *all* of it. You may not have had permission to feel your feelings, but you do now. In fact, it's imperative to your happiness and wellbeing that you feel your feelings. I wish there were a magic wand we could wave to make them vanish, but as a human being, you have emotions, so as the saying goes: *The only way out is through.*

Step 3. Create Comfort for Yourself

Grief may need a different release than anger. Anger may need big, explosive movements to clear. Grief, on the other hand, may need comfort, nurturing, and love. You can imagine wrapping a blanket of light around your heart for comforting support. Or you can physically wrap yourself in an actual blanket, lay on the ground, and let the earth hold you in your grief. Breathe into it and have a deep cry if needed.

Step 4. Connection

It may be appropriate to connect with a friend or therapist who can truly hear you. If you are processing your own grief, it may be helpful to receive some validation, talk out your feelings, or feel that someone can empathize with you.

Step 5. Allow

Allowing what grief is there to be there is a gentle way of not controlling the process. If you can lean back and surrender your hurt and pain to the Divine, without judging yourself for having it, you are creating movement in the heart for relief. Allowing includes deeper breathing and opening up to the Divine for more support. There may not be a fast solution to get you out of feeling grief, but the mind cannot make that happen anyway. Grief is a process of allowing, surrendering control, and feeling the emotions.

Here is a way you can support yourself in allowing:

Close your eyes and lean back into your body. Feel a waterfall of light behind you, and lean into it. Take some deep breaths. Breathe that light into the back of your heart, allowing the Divine light to come

CHAPTER 7 - HEALING GUIDE

in and support you. When you exhale, give up to the Divine, through the back of your heart, the hurt, pain, and the whole situation you are grieving over. Give it up to the Divine. Inhale, draw the light into the back of your heart, and allow Divine support to help heal you. Exhale, release the pain, offer it up, and let it go out the back (or sometimes front) of the heart.

Step 6. Reprogram

Reprogramming may depend on who or what you are grieving. In some situations, the step of allowing may be all you need right now to soothe, heal, and provide comfort.

If you are clearing old grief from the distant past, it's possible to grieve all your past suffering and then choose to live from an open, courageous, and loving heart. In this case, reprogramming may be appropriate for you.

What is the opposite of grief for you? Your answer may be different from someone else's. What comes to you is exactly what you need to fill the space created from the fear releasing. As I mentioned earlier, in energy work, it's advised to replace a negative feeling, image, or word with a positive one. Otherwise, the space is unclaimed and negativity can refill it. In the case of grief, the feelings are not necessarily negative. Sure, it doesn't feel great to feel sorrow, but grief can be a doorway to a spiritual heart opening. By letting your human self process the sadness, and letting your spirit choose a power to live from, what occurs is a strengthening of the spiritual heart. A strong spiritual heart then supports a healthy human heart.

So declare what intention you would like to live from, and breathe it into that space. It can be a new belief, such as "I am open" or "I courageously live from the intuition in my heart." It can even be the feeling of presence and love. It can also be a color or an image that depicts how you want to live in your body. Additionally, there could be a quote, song, poem, or other wording that would speak to the *power* of your spirit. These words might also mirror what you want when you think of what your life will be like on the other side of fear.

Step 7. Support Yourself

With grief clearing, clouds of fogginess and emotions disappear. What results is a deeper connection to Self and Spirit. So tune into what your body needs so you can take care of yourself. Self-care goes deeper than a bubble bath and pampering (although those are appropriate forms of self-care). Caring for Self means tuning into your heart, soul, and intuition, and asking yourself what you need to support yourself during this time of processing grief. It may take some conscious effort on your part to live from your new intention, but stay connected to your heart's intuition about what you need. Sometimes, music, singing, hugging, laughing, or just breathing can really help you feel connected to your soul.

Once you've felt the grief settle, your spirit can come through with the higher meaning, vision, or purpose for your life, as well as insights related to your life situation. When grieving, many people ask, "Why did this happen?" What's important to know is that, in the moment, no reason will make this feeling of grief go away any faster, and you won't get clarity to that question when you're in grief. Once the grief has passed and you can feed your soul by tending to what you need, your heart will mature and the "Why?" question may make sense. It also may take time.

The Importance of Emotional Release

The majority of blockage in our energetic body is stuck emotions.

With energy healing, an emotional *release* is a good thing. An emotional *reaction* means there is more for you to consider in this area. It is important to know the difference between releasing and reacting. You will know because a release will resolve with a sense of peace, while a reaction will trail with feelings of regret, guilt, or a sense that things are still unresolved.

What is Releasing?

Releasing is a process that can follow any time you have a physical, emotional, or energetic shift in your body. Most likely, you have experienced releasing throughout your life through crying, yelling, dancing, singing, breathing, exercising, etc. Releasing is a big part of the healing work.

The following information will further support you when you are going through a release. With energy healing, you are working in the Divine Realm to move large energies that may have held you back, have kept you stuck, or no longer serve you. Energy, cells, and DNA are all connected. (I recommend watching the movie *What the Bleep Do We Know!?* It talks about cellular reactions to energy in our bodies in terms of Quantum Physics.) Once energies clear, a healing takes place, and your body reacts to that shift. Your cells transform, and your chemical makeup responds in turn. The emotional shift in your body after a healing may help you feel lighter or more relaxed. The more you clear, the greater the changes in your body.

Releasing takes place during and in the days following a healing. This is a crucial time for shifting. It has taken our whole life to be who we are, and if we are carrying blocks that have become part of our chemical makeup, most likely, a single clearing may only address one layer of what needs to be healed. I mentioned that the energy in our cells shifts. As that shift occurs, other layers are stirred up, or a stored memory in the body surfaces. Because emotions are stored in our cellular makeup and tissues, as the cells shift, emotions release. It is very natural to have a wonderful healing followed by an experience of mixed emotions days later. Here is where the release process becomes very important. If you do not release these emotions, they stay exactly where they are in your body reducing the overall effect of any healing you may have received.

Breathing

The most crucial part of a release is to breathe. We are so busy these days that we often take care of everyone and everything else in our lives except ourselves. Be still and breathe deeply. Let your breath cleanse you so you may start your day refreshed with new oxygen. You may want to research different breathing techniques such as breath of fire, three-part breath, or variations on belly breathing, which are wonderful cleansing techniques. In the process, you may feel both heavy and lighter emotions, including:

Heavy Emotions: Anger, Sadness, Grief, Jealousy, Doubt, Hate, Frustration, Resentment, Questioning Life, or a tingling in your body.

Lighter Emotions: Peace, Happiness, Joy, Love, Expansiveness, Connectedness, Openness, Being Powerful, Inspired, and more....

How Does a Release Happen for Me?

Because everyone is different, release is individual and occurs in different ways. Honor yourself and do what you can to address the heavy emotions that want to come out. Also, notice if you resist the lighter emotions, such as joy, peace, and happiness. Sometimes, there is a release of the heavier emotions in order to feel the lighter emotions.

Below is a list of activities you can do to help move through the emotions of a release. Before you begin any activity, first set your intention that the activity is to release whatever emotion you are going through. Feel the emotion to the fullest. Feeling it completely will help it move faster.

- ♥ **Get out into Nature!** Getting out into nature is *very* important. It is amazing how much clarity you get from a walk in the hills or on the beach. Nature grounds, centers, and balances you, and it connects you to the rest of creation of which you are a part: Creation! Just to have your mind calm will help you get some perspective so you can come back to your routine with a fresh outlook.
- ♥ Exercise: run, bike, walk, play a sport, etc.
- ♥ Meditate.
- ♥ Practice yoga.
- ♥ Punch a punching bag or pillow to release anger/frustration.
- ♥ Throw rocks in the ocean/lake to release anger/frustration. (Saltwater will purify the emotion in the rock.)
- ♥ Talk to an understanding friend.
- ♥ Go out and have a great time doing something fun!
- ♥ Be creative!
- ♥ Grounding: Establish your grounding chord, and send the emotion down your grounding chord with the intention that it is being released from your body and will be purified in the center of the earth.
- ♥ Deep Breathing: Blow out the emotion!
- ♥ Use colors to heal: purple, pink, or white light. Feel free to use colors that feel right for you. Wrap yourself in them.
- ♥ Go on a day trip somewhere.
- ♥ Explore creative outlets: music, dance, singing, painting, sculpture, creating, etc.

- ♥ Get a massage. I work with some wonderful massage therapists, and I would be happy to refer one to you if you would like. Massage is a wonderful way to access the emotion in a deeper way through physical contact.
- ♥ Acupuncture: Getting Chi flowing in your body will also help move the emotions out and restore your vitality.
- ♥ Baths: with sea salt, herbs, or oils—very healing!
- ♥ Flower Essences/Herbs: These can help support your healing process.
- ♥ Healthy Food: Our diet can impede emotional release when we are not eating consciously, while nutrient-dense food can support our systems through the releasing.

- ♥ Prayer/Intention/Manifesting

- ♥ Cooking/Baking

These are just a few activities that will help you to release emotions. There are many more, and because everyone is different, you will want to tune in to your own intuition to determine which ones would be right for you.

Healing for Your Soul

Healing on an emotional level will take you through the story of the past to unblock old emotions. Healing on the soul level is about listening, nurturing, and attending to what your soul is asking of you. Tending to your soul requires faith, trust, and listening to the voice of your own intuition. It also includes considering your soul's choice to be here in this life to help you live in connection to the Divine.

As you move through the Stage of Healing, your soul will need *sourcing*. To source yourself means to give yourself what your soul needs so your body can let it go. Some people source themselves by going to the ocean, doing their art, or listening to a talk by a thought leader. Whatever your sourcing is, it is something your soul tells you that you need. To know what your Soul needs, you need to be familiar with that inner voice. You do know that voice. It's the one that speaks softly and gives you inner direction and guidance.

Sometimes, however, the Ego gets in the way of the intuitive voice. As discussed earlier, the Ego voice is the noise of the emotions and belief systems having their own party in your mind. Your intuition is your Soul's voice in union with the Divine. If your Ego voice is louder than your intuitive voice, you need to ground yourself. Your wounds may be talking—not your intuition. Grounding is a process of allowing your energy to relax, slow down, and become connected to the slower pace of the earth's natural vibration. When you ground yourself, your body settles. When your body settles, then your mind settles.

Some people are chronically ungrounded. In such cases, some deep healing is needed in the lower power centers. When we have blocks in the lower chakras, the energy automatically rises too high in the body. If it's been that way for a long time, then that feeling is normal, yet it is chronic ungroundedness. It is very hard to feel the soul's voice when the energetic system is chronically ungrounded. It is possible to work on grounding, yet it will take facing some old wounds to move the blocked energy.

So how do you ground and connect to your intuition?

To answer this question, we will delve a bit deeper into the topics of grounding, intuition, faith, meditation, the energetic body, and the path of the soul. All of this information supports heart expansion and a greater understanding of how to connect to intuition and Divine wisdom.

Grounding

Grounding is the most important tool for healing and connecting to your intuition. As human beings, we are made from the same particles that are in nature. We are a part of nature. The more closely connected we live with nature, the closer we are to the source of our natural state. If we eat food that was just picked from the garden and prepared by our own hands, we are grounding through food. If we take the time to unplug from technology and decompress the nervous system in nature, that is grounding. Grounding is letting the deep current syncopate with Mother Earth's rhythm. I have seen in myself and others that when a connection to the earth is absent, sometimes grief occurs in the home-coming to the ground.

When we unwind, it puts the entire body into balance. More conscious choices can be made, the body heals, the heart relaxes, and the mind stops racing. Grounding is how we connect to our soul. When the body is grounded, the soul is grounded in the body. I like to imagine that my soul takes a deep seat in my body when I am consciously practicing grounding. There are many ways to ground. Here are some suggestions:

Ways we ground:

- ♥ Slow down the inner pace.
- ♥ Eat healthy, digestible, nutrient-rich foods that balance the system.
- ♥ Connect to Mother Earth: spend time decompressing in nature, and allow the natural world to bring you into balance.
- ♥ Visualize a Grounding Cord. (See description below.)
- ♥ Sleep

The Grounding Cord

Visualizations can really help when healing from a soul-level. I recommend using visualizations as needed, as often as you can. Part of your brain doesn't know the difference between visualizing and a real action, so the body will benefit from using visualization. For example, if you have a stomach ache, visualize healing light in that area of the body. See what happens to your body, mind, and soul when you use a visualization to shift how you feel.

The Grounding Cord can be utilized in a similar way. It is a line of energy that anchors us to the earth. You can visualize your grounding cord as a beam of light or a tree-trunk-like image with roots that sprout into the earth's core. When you visualize your Grounding Cord, you can see it connected from your hips to the earth's center.

Breathe deeply and let your body relax into that support. At the same time, let the earth energy rise up through the backside of your Grounding Cord and let yourself be fueled by a strong current of earth energy. It will actually relax you when you feel the earth energy rise up to support you. This is a meditation. The more you practice the meditation, the more strongly you will feel grounded.

The Grounding Cord is also a wonderful depository for the unwanted energy that releases from your body during clearing and energy healing work. You can breathe into the places in your body where you feel blocked and keep breathing into it. Then, let the energy release down your Grounding Cord. The cord will take that energy to the earth's center where it will be transformed into pure light.

In order to tune into yourself, grounding and slowing down are extremely important. You may not get accurate information if you are ungrounded. Racing internally and being in a fantasy are both forms of being ungrounded. So be sure to ground with the grounding cord and meditations, as well as with any suggested grounding method or your own methods.

Intuition

Intuition is the voice of your spirit guiding you consciously through life. You may know your intuition as the little voice inside, gut feelings, or intuitive hits. These are all ways you experience the transmission of higher wisdom through, or into, your human experience. Intuition is the communication between Spirit and our human self.

The true intuitive voice comes when we are still and quiet. It may say such things as "Be Still" or "Yes!" It may not give you long paragraphs of information. Your soul's messages are to aid you in the present moment. Everything you need to know about feeling safe in the future is provided by being in the present moment. From there, you're intuition speaks to you. To hear fully your intuition, you have to come into the present moment. So allow yourself the time to go deep, tune in, be still, listen, and feel. Going deeper within is the advancement in your intuition.

Intuition can be felt in various places in the body. The heart is the power center where we feel our yearnings and desires for happiness and fulfillment. Our soul leads us through our heart. The Solar Plexus is where we may feel those gut feelings or that deep knowing. The phrase "I know in my gut I should have taken that right turn" is an example of an intuitive "hit" which can resonate in the body's core. Intuition in the lower abdomen is a sign of danger or that something is wrong. The body is the best indicator that intuitive information is trying to come through. We may get suddenly tired, shut down, have a stomach ache, or even feel confusion if our body is telling us something is not right. Listening to those gut feelings and body reactions to situations is listening to your intuition.

To tune into your intuition, it may be helpful to know where some of the intuitive voices comes from.

The Inner Child: The most reliable aspect of your intuition is your inner child. Much of how we operate subconsciously comes from the inner child consciousness trying to get needs met. So one of the first voices to get really acquainted with is your inner child. Tune into your inner child in your heart or belly area and listen to what he or she wants. If you are doing something that is not good for you, he or she will let you know! It may happen through emotional reaction or physical symptoms. Tune in and ask this voice often what he or she is needing. It may be something like attention or comfort. Meet the need of your inner child and your need to seek it externally may subside.

Your Heart: Your Heart Chakra is where you may feel the spiritual truth of a situation. It may be conflicting sometimes with what your ego wants. Many people say, "Part of me wants to do this…and the other part of me wants to do this other option." When this happens, tune in. Does your soul want to do one thing, but your mind is pro-grammed to follow expectations? Is your soul's voice in conflict with doing the "safe" or "right" thing? Sometimes those "safe" or "right" things are actually fear-based thoughts taught to us. Maybe they were needed in our youth to help us have boundaries and containers. How-ever, it's up to you to live with what's true in the present moment and decide whether those old ways of staying safe are really true in the present. To determine what's true, notice what your ego is saying and notice what your heart is saying. Separate out the voices. Then deeply meditate on your heart. Stay there until the light and power of your heart comes in clear to you with a true sense or voice.

Your Gut: Gut feelings come from your Second or Third Chakras. They are most likely feelings, but they can be voices that sometimes come from deep within. Gut feelings are gut feelings, and we all know what happens when we deny those feelings. It's important to have a clean "gut" nutritionally, emotionally, and energetically for your gut feelings to be true. Sometimes, people's gut feelings protect them from potential danger, but if fear is dominant in this area as a wound, there may be a tendency to be worried or fearful of everything. These are not true "gut" feelings. True gut feelings are deeper. Truth is deeper. Clean up the "gut" to strengthen the power of intuition here. Having a healthy digestive track is important. Take probiotics and digestive enzymes, and most importantly, eat living foods that are clean, organic, and rich in natural enzymes for a healthy "gut brain" and intuition.

The Divine Messages: These messages come through the Divine realm from spirit guides, angels, and the light of God. They are downloaded to us regularly, whether or not we are aware of them. To receive these messages, the prayer channel needs to be open. For some people, the prayer channel has been open since birth; they hear these messages easily, and it's a gift to have that connection open. For others, healing may need to occur throughout a lifetime in order for the Divine Source and the source within to make contact. It also can be cultivated through meditation and active prayer. In the next section, Divine Communication, we go further into opening up this connection to allow these messages to come through.

Faith and the Divine Communication

Living with faith is living with a relationship to the Divine. Faith elevates consciousness because you are engaging a spiritual backbone that gives your soul confidence. When you have faith, you live life sourced and connected. Faith also gives you the feeling of being guided and protected in this life so you know you are not alone, but a contributor to a larger mission.

When you have faith, you are willing to invite the light of God into your human struggles and hand over what you cannot control. You are willing to be infused with spiritual Grace so you are not "doing" this life alone. This connection in the body happens through a channel of light called the Pillar of Light. This is your prayer channel and the pillar through which you experience Divine communication. When this pillar is not engaged, light cannot enter the spiritual center of the crown chakra or the heart. Then feelings exist of negativity, doubt, fear, being lost, and living disconnected from meaning and purpose. Divine communication is what engages the soul with something bigger than yourself. Intuition is not only about hearing ourselves, but about accessing the bigger picture.

The Pillar of Light

The Pillar of Light in the body is also known as the Susumna Channel. It is the primary meridian that runs along the length of the spine and through your core. It begins at the crown chakra and ends at the pelvic floor, and then it merges with the Grounding Cord. The pillar is the pipeline in us through which Grace flows. When the pillar is blocked or bent, we may feel off. Nothing should be in the pillar but our own light and essence. However, deep core issues are those life experiences that impact us so profoundly that the issues reside in the core pillar. When we go through our healing process and work through our core issues, emotions and energy move out of the pillar to the body's periphery, no longer being core issues. The further an issue has moved out, the less impacted we feel by it.

For healing, you can run Divine Light or Grace through the crown of your head and through the Pillar, as if you are daily showering yourself off. The more you visualize yourself taking in Divine Grace and letting this pillar expand, the more you will glow. Of course, this process may bring up emotions and wounds to clear, but when you move through those blocks, light can freely flow through you.

To give you a better perspective on the Pillar of Light, I want to share an experience I had with my pillar:

The first time I felt the pillar of light in my body, I was living in Boulder, Colorado. I was a daily hiker and was hiking near the Flatirons, a place where I often communed with God, but I didn't really know that was what I was doing at the time.

One day, I felt this strong line of energy from the crown of my head to my tailbone, and I had an omnipotent knowingness of the Pillar of Light. I then heard what felt like a voice from God say to me, "Visualize this every day and you will be healed." Now, looking back, I can't believe I wasn't skeptical or didn't think, *Yeah, right; it's that easy?* But I wasn't skeptical at all. The power of that knowingness in my body and my relationship to that pillar was beyond words.

So I did it. I visualized that pillar every day for one year. I was young, probably twenty-three years old. That year, I had many divine openings that set the foundation for my being a healer in the world. What the voice didn't clarify at the time was that "healing" meant hurting sometimes—feeling pain, forgiving, facing fears, taking risks, and to quit whining and complaining, etc. It wasn't this amazing, great, blissful-feeling time. That's not healing.

I was willing to face it all. At times, I would experience the pillar in my body, and at the same time, be having a very uncomfortable issue with a friend. Then other times, the emotions would take over and I would cry and go to the depths of it. But even through these healing releases, as I called them, I would feel my pillar even stronger in my body. It got so strong that my posture changed. My spine got straighter and my heart lifted.

During this time, I navigated through the twists and turns of life. The image of the pillar does not imply rigidity. In fact, it's the opposite. The pillar is light and the presence of life-force energy. You can have plenty of life-force energy in your body, but if you infuse that pillar with the light of the Divine, you are turbo-charging your body with a powerful surge of wisdom and faith. To be clear about this, you are not taking energy from God to put into your body so you are wise and powerful. The only way this connection will open for you is if you are willing to listen, let go, and surrender to the power of the Divine. If you are afraid of God because of religious associations you don't agree with, then you owe it to yourself to let go of all preconceptions and reintroduce yourself to God with a clean slate. You may need to redefine what God means to you because until you are able to release shame and association to religious dogma, you have not truly found the Divine, Spirit, the Light, Life Force, God, or whatever you want to call it. Once you truly feel this power, this grace, there is no mistake that you are connected. Your body knows this connection even though your mind doesn't. So if you're still struggling with the word *God*, there may be more letting go to do.

Having a prayer practice and visualizing your Pillar of Light are ways you stay connected to the Divine in your day-to-day life. Life becomes much easier when you engage with this flow.

Some ways you can work with the Pillar of Light this week:

- ♥ Close your eyes and visualize your Pillar of Light.
- ♥ Draw a picture of what your Pillar of Light looks like to you.
- ♥ Run light through the center of your body.
- ♥ Pray from any chakra through this channel.

This week, work with strengthening the Pillar of Light in your body so you resonate with more Divine Light.

Prayer

To have a regular prayer practice will strengthen the flow of Grace in your life. I approach prayer the same way I approach meditation. When I sit to pray, I go into a meditative state and I breathe. I feel the Pillar of Light in my body engage. I feel my Grounding Cord. I feel my crown chakra open up to the Divine. I continue to breathe into my heart. Then I offer up whatever my heart wants to say. I don't think about it; I just let my heart speak. Sometimes, my prayer is to offer gratitude for everything I have been given in my life. Other times, my prayer is to ask for strength, healing, or help with something I am struggling with. I also pray for my clients, other people in my life who are in need, and sometimes for the planet. I'm sharing my experience with prayer as an example, but you can establish a prayer practice that works for you.

Consistent prayer and meditation will strengthen the Pillar of Light, as well as your heart, and create a strong relationship to the Divine and higher consciousness. Additionally, in order for intuition truly to open up, this pillar needs to be established and maintained through all the power centers in the body. This happens by means of prayer and the infusion of light consciousness through the body. So prayer is not something outside of you. Prayer comes from your heart and soul to the Divine.

It is natural to wonder: If prayer is the tool, to whom am I praying? God? The Universe? Divine Love? Whom or what you pray to is your own subjective relationship, and it needs to be felt and experienced within you. For me, all these words are synonyms with slightly different vibrational experiences. What they have in common is the capacity to bring access to a Higher Power. The word "God" can be loaded, depending on one's religious experience, so it becomes important then to separate religion from spirituality in order to heal any unnecessary charge around the word God.

The words you use for spiritual connection are a very personal choice. If it feels unsure at all, perhaps you can start with Divine Love, the Earth Mother, or the Universe, if that helps you at least establish the connection. Your intuition will increase dramatically once you establish and cultivate this connection.

Meditation

Meditation is a form of prayer and connection to Self. Many ways exist to meditate, and many books have been written on meditation and meditation practices. There is no right or wrong way to meditate. For me personally, having a strong yoga background, I follow meditation I learn through my yoga trainings. Other people follow Buddhist or Christian methods of meditating. Just as the word "love" can be said in many different languages, there are many different paths to quieting your mind and connecting you to Self and the Divine when meditating.
Meditation calms the excess energy moving around in the body. Therefore, the mind quiets. Some people say they can't meditate because

the mind just races. In these cases, a deep need exists for grounding practices or even movement. Walking meditation is an option. Some other ways to meditate are: focusing on breath, counting, visualizing a flame, guided meditation, yoga nidra, and focusing on the word "love" or "peace."

If you are new to meditating, try these steps:

- ♥ Find a comfortable, quiet place where you will be free from distractions.
- ♥ Take some deep breaths, and ground through your Grounding Cord, allowing your body to settle.
- ♥ Close your eyes, slow your pace, and lean back into your Pillar of Light. Feel it at your mid-line. You will automatically center and possibly feel your posture shift.
- ♥ Breathe. Settle your body.
- ♥ It can take up to ten minutes before your body really feels settled into meditation, so be mindful not to rush.
- ♥ With your eyes closed, feel the light of the Divine pouring love into the top of your head. Let it fill your Pillar of Light. Breathe. Let your entire being receive the light of love.
- ♥ Stay here with this feeling as long as you can. Even if you think you can only stay in this meditation for five minutes, stay five minutes longer.
- ♥ Upon completion, add a prayer or intention for yourself and for your day.
- ♥ Allow yourself to be filled completely with this pure sense of light and radiance.
- ♥ Enter into your day or end your day knowing you have just received a healing.

Energetic Body

Learning more about the energetic anatomy can help meditation. If your consciousness just grazes the surface of your inner being, it may be difficult to settle and even connect to clear intuition.

Understanding that power centers exist in the body and visualizing your energetic anatomy can be helpful with tuning in. It's important to know how your consciousness works in each of the power centers. When your consciousness has visited these areas of your internal landscape, you will be able to visit these areas of consciousness again in your meditations.

Beneath the surface of our physical skin and organs is our energetic anatomy. The energetic anatomy includes chakras (or power centers) as well as information on our mental, emotional, spiritual, and physical states of being. The chakras carry information on who we are and how we operate in the world. Sensitive people can perceive the chakras' information within them.

According to ancient Indian belief, the human body is divided into two parts: the physical and the spiritual (soul). In each human being, the spiritual body contains the chakras, which in Sanskrit means a "wheel" or a "disk." Although there are thousands of chakras, seven main chakras are located along the central line of the body from the spine to the top of the head. Chakras provide information, such as body shape, the glandular process, chronic physical ailments, thoughts, and behaviors. According to ancient Indian thought, the universal life force flows through the top of the head and down the chakras, influencing and nurturing our body, soul, and mind. Each chakra has a different frequency and pace of vibration, a different color, and a different symbol and sound. And each chakra needs to function independently in its own correct frequency. When a chakra is not vibrating or moving properly and is deviating from its regular frequency, it indicates a problem.

When healing from a soul level, the chakras need to be observed and understood correctly in order to find the exact problem lying within them so they can heal properly. How do you heal energetically? One example is bringing breath and awareness into the area where there is blockage and setting intention that it will clear. However, returning the body to a natural state of rest and desensitization is a wonderful way to let the body naturally unwind and heal.

From a chakra perspective, the chakras absorb and transmit energy to and from the natural world, including nature, people, and universal life-force energy. When the chakras are charged with healthy life-force energy, they illuminate and become empowered. Nature itself is a powerful healing tool for balancing the chakras and healing the body. Being in nature will decompress the mind, relax the body, and channel all the natural energy toward healing the person seeking help.

Ancient belief says all energy can be harnessed and directed based on the healer's intentions. The healer, however, must be in alignment with the Divine life force and the natural world for healing to occur. As the body relaxes, the chakras can naturally realign and center.

As mentioned before, many chakra books are out there, including mine: *Energy Healing Through the Chakras: A Guide to Self-Healing.* I will offer an overview of the chakras for reference, but since the chakras are vast and so much has been written on them, I've refrained from going into detail about them in this book.

Chakras:

First Chakra: Located at the base of the spine. Relates to survival instincts, basic needs, tribal beliefs, security, abundance, physical health, and grounding on the physical plane.

Second Chakra: Located at the sacrum. Relates to sexuality, creativity, partnerships, how we feel our emotions and the depths of our emotions, feminine energy, intuition, and going with the flow of life.

Third Chakra: Located at the solar plexus of the body. Relates to personal power, confidence, identity, personal boundaries, how we digest life, and how we manage power. It's the masculine power center for taking action, manifesting, and expressing will.

Fourth Chakra: Located at the heart center in the middle of the chest. Relates to love, self-love, compassion, peace, and union with the Divine. Our purpose, wants, and desires are felt like a calling here in the heart.

Fifth Chakra: Located at the throat. It is the chakra for communication, speaking our truth, expression of will and creativity, saying yes or no to possibilities, and listening.

Sixth Chakra: Located at the third eye center. Relates to seeing intuitively, visualizing, ability to perceive, and seeing the optimum potential for living life.

Seventh Chakra: Located a few inches above the crown of the head. Relates to spiritual awareness and connection to Source, the flow of life, wisdom, and faith that all is being taken care of.

Cheat Sheet

In my Healer Training Program, a student jokingly said to me, "Wendy, give me the cheat sheet. I just want the cheat sheet to all this healing stuff." Laughing, I said, "Okay! I will write you a cheat sheet." I called this the cheat sheet, but in actuality, practicing these three acts clears energy and old karma and connects you to the Divine instantly. They are:

Forgiveness

Gratitude

Love

If you can authentically and truthfully feel these three powers, then you will heal faster. If you still have pain, you have to deal with the pain. Why? Because you can't forgive fully if you're still angry, you won't be grateful if your heart is still hurting, and fear will block love. So you can process your wounds in order to feel forgiveness, gratitude, and love, or you can practice feeling forgiveness, gratitude, and love in order to heal.

Either way, these three acts of power are the fastest access to your Divine connection, prayer, grace, joy, and wellbeing. If you are not ready to forgive, feel grateful, or feel love, you may still need to go back through the Healing Guide to process harboring or stuck emotions.

How do you know when you are healed?

The bigger question is: Are we ever healed? We are an evolving consciousness, which means that as we evolve and life around us evolves, we will be faced with reflections that challenge us to live our fullest potential. There is no endgame here. Living the journey of loving who you are is the healing. As you embrace more love and acceptance for your perfections and imperfections, you increasingly expand your heart field. This process allows you to have a different relationship to your difficult past experiences and wounds.

You know you have experienced healing when you look back on a wounded time in your life and you have a completely transformed reaction to it. You are no longer angry, fearful, or upset. As human beings, we have emotions. How you relate to your emotions determines how well you will heal. How you relate to your past after processing the emotions is where you see transformation. You can build strength and resources within by healing your wounds so you can live your life from a completely different molding.

REFLECTION QUESTIONS

Theme:
Healing Guide Progress

Use the following questions below to discuss how the Healing Guide was useful to you.

As you explore, be concise, to the point, and acknowledge the feelings you had at the time. If emotions are still present for you about the past, name those emotions.

Consider the Following Questions:

♥ Was the Healing Guide helpful? If so, how? If not, why?

♥ How did you follow a process of unpacking emotions? Describe the process you used.

♥ Did you have any revelations, clearings, or celebrations while practicing the exercises?

♥ Did you notice any resistance, defensiveness, or fear come up around looking at an issue or emotion? If so, how did you work with it?

♥ Will you be able to return to this Healing Guide whenever you need a reminder on how to process emotions?

♥ Have there been any changes in your life now that you have more tools to work with your emotions?

♫ **GUIDED MEDITATION AUDIO**

Log in to www.SchoolofIntuitiveStudies.com through the Expanding Your Heart link to receive your guided meditation titled "Healing Old Emotions Meditation."

Chapter 8

CONTEMPLATIVE BEING

"Now is the time to know that all that you do is sacred....
Now is the time for you to deeply compute the impossibility
that there is anything but grace."
— Hafiz

Contemplative Being is the experience of living in connection with the True Self and with the Divine, and making use of the supportive coping skills, spiritual maturation, and increased awareness we gain after having passed through the stages of the Initial Heart Opening, Chaos, and Healing. Arriving at the stage of Contemplative Being, we find ourselves spiritually strong, connected to the Divine, living from awareness, and in possession of skills and strategies that enable us to live meaningful lives.

The word "contemplative" has been used to describe being in spiritual communion with the Divine. In the Christian tradition, for instance, Contemplative Prayer, or The Path of Contemplation, refers to being in a spiritually meditative experience. For me, Contemplative Being means: Experiencing a relationship between the light in the heart and

Divine Source in a way that facilitates and maintains an awakened consciousness. It does not mean perfection, the absence of pain, or feeling superior. It does mean that as we move through our human lives, we experience a spiritual connection, and we have a sense of being in union with the Divine and of service to others and the world as we share our light.

In the stage of Contemplative Being, we are aware that we are not the sum total of our emotions, nor are we the reactions we have to our emotions. Our Heart has opened and we have compassion and Self-Love. We know how to care for ourselves during a trigger. We know when something feels out of alignment and we correct it. We take responsibility for how our life is unfolding. Our needs have typically shifted, and we find ourselves needing less because we are fulfilled by something greater than material possessions or worldly achievements. Our behavior flows from a life steeped in love, rather than one that perpetuates harm. We may have a spiritual or soul-filled practice that grounds us, and we tend to our Soul. Inner showers of light to heal and clear energetically become just as necessary as external showers of water to cleanse the body. We know the difference between being centered and un-centered. We want to live lives full of meaning and purpose.

In Contemplative Being, we experience the Spiritually Open Heart. When the noise of the body-mind becomes quiet, and we are sourced through spiritual awareness, the heart opens in a way that could evoke tears, joy, elation, celebration, big expansion feelings, etc. Consciousness has touched the center of the heart, allowing the light of Grace to enter.

If we are still in Healing, can we also be in the stage of Contemplative Being? Absolutely. In fact, Healing can gently guide us to this fourth stage and support the Spiritual Heart opening. The same response applies to Chaos—can Chaos occur when you are in Contemplative Being? Absolutely. Below is the story of a woman who went through a painful heart opening, emotional chaos, and turned to meditation for healing. Then she shocked her husband by confronting him with love instead of anger.

Kathy's Story

Kathy's husband had had an affair. When she found out about it, she thought it had been going on for about three to five months. Upon her discovery, she chose not to confront her husband right away. Instead, she began to meditate. Kathy meditated on her own heart. She meditated on her pain. She meditated on the history of their marriage, what went wrong, and what was right. She meditated on her feelings of betrayal and her overwhelming devastation. She did this for four more months, knowing that he was continuing this affair. Kathy was fully aware of this the whole time, but she stayed very connected to herself, until she couldn't wait anymore and it was time to confront him.

When she confronted him, she was in her center, clear, and calm. She wasn't a victim. She wasn't blaming. She just very calmly relayed what she knew and she let him know how hurt she was. She was able to talk about her feelings without projecting her feelings at him. The result was that he was shocked by how calm she was. Because she had processed her feelings so much beforehand, he held the guilt. He couldn't become defensive because there was nothing for him to defend. He took responsibility. Kathy chose to be in her heart for herself. As a result, they decided to continue to work on the marriage.

This story is an example of what happens when you turn inward in the midst of great devastation. In Contemplative Being, there is consciousness and a strong intuition that comes through on how to handle a situation. This woman could have ignored her inner voice, but that would have put her into further Chaos because she may have just reacted and acted out toward him, which would have caused a painful battle. Instead, she decided to pray and meditate, and she found the spiritual strength to open doors within that she never knew were there. As a result, she maintained her power and continued to do what felt right to her. Hers was a Spiritually Expanded Heart.

The Spiritually Expanded Heart

You may recall the concept of the Sacred Heart discussed earlier in this book. In some traditions, the heart is considered the seat of the soul. We are in alignment with our truth when we live from the sacred center of our heart, something that requires a great deal of responsibility and discipline. Living from the heart means facing the contradictions that may be present in your life, such as admitting to yourself that you overeat even though you think you have a balanced relationship to food. It means admitting that you don't take care of your body even though you tell yourself and others that you do, and it means admitting to yourself that you are not actually happy, although you tell others that you are. Entering your heart means you are ready to see yourself clearly, and from that clarity, you are willing to love yourself and God in equal measure, to such an extent that you perceive no separation between you and the rest of creation. From this place of seeing the Divine within you, you also see the Divine within others. As your relationship with yourself grows deeper and gets stronger, so do your relationships with others.

We never have to force the heart open: It will naturally blossom as we work on healing ourselves. While it might take years, the opening is consistent enough that we will experience moments of awakening along the entire journey.

From an energetic perspective, a Spiritually Expanded Heart includes a component of Divine Grace entering into the backside of the Heart Chakra. It is at the backside of the heart that we meditate on questions such as: *What does God ask of me in this world? What is my truth, my mission, my purpose?* We connect to our Divine calling when we allow ourselves to be open to answers about purpose and meaning, knowing such answers come to us through deep meditation and transmission of Divine energy through the backside of the heart chakra.

People who are givers, nurturers, or caretakers are associated with predominantly generous and open-hearted qualities. However, when giving and receiving occur only through the front side of the heart, and no consciousness, light, or prayer is entering through the back side, the giver will often feel depleted, and even resentful, because the love and care she offers exclusively from the front are, in fact, conditional. Conditional love means that we give with an expectation of a reward or in-kind payment, although the requirement for validation is rarely, if ever, articulated. What that means is that, conditionally, I give to you, and if you don't give back to me, I become resentful and angry, and I remain unfulfilled. Calling Divine light in to the backside of the heart supports us in feeling fulfilled, thus reducing our need for external sources of love and validation; instead, we allow ourselves to be sourced by the spiritual light behind us. From this place of fullness, we can give to others, confident that the Divine has our back.

Having a spiritually open heart includes feeling expansive love for self, others, Spirit, and for the planet. To a spiritually open heart, love is not about finding a life partner, or otherwise looking outside of ourselves for gratification so we can feel secure and successful. A spiritually open heart experiences love as a state of being—Contemplative Being.

Spiritual Heart Opening Meditation

Use the following meditation to begin your journey toward an opening of your spiritual heart. An audio version of this recording is available at www.SchoolofIntuitiveStudies.com.

Take off your shoes, as if you were preparing to walk into a sacred temple.

Prepare to enter the temple of your heart by leaving your busy mind outside because you can't think your way into your heart; you have to feel your way there. Don't worry, though, because your soul knows the way; your soul has been there before, and it will take you there again this time. Your soul knows what it's like to be in your heart. Your soul remembers the way and can easily guide you through all your fears.

Close your eyes and enter this meditation by seeing that your soul has been busy looking on the outside for answers, comfort, and importance. Visualize your soul taking off its shoes and walking into the center of your heart. Once it reaches the center, close the temple doors.

Sit there. Breathe. Slow your breath down. It could take more than ten minutes before your body settles, so don't be quick to get up. Become acquainted with the inside of your heart because you will need to return here many times before your awareness of this place feels comfortable and familiar to you.

Get used to the silence forming a backdrop for your chattering mind. Let the silence be a blue sky and your thoughts be clouds that float in and out of your awareness. Don't judge yourself for having thoughts; just watch them float in and out like passing clouds. Over time, the clouds will pass more infrequently.

Now, lean back into a waterfall of light. Feel that the light enters into the backside of your heart chakra, warming your spine and shoulder blades. It flows into the center of your heart and fills your entire chest with a sensation of light, Divine presence, love, and Grace. Breathe in the light.... Exhale and expand the light through the temple of your heart.

Remain here in the temple of your heart with all its chambers. Your soul, a brilliant light, has a whispering voice that echoes in your heart's chambers. If you quiet yourself so much that the whispers become the loudest sounds you hear, you know you are sitting in the temple of your heart.

From this place, you will embark on a journey where great spiritual unfolding will occur. You have not arrived at your final destination; rather you are at the beginning. In this sacred stillness, you are more connected with God than you have ever been. In this temple, you offer your recompense, your gratitude, your moral conviction, your suffering, your appreciation for the life you have been given. Here is where you truly shift and heal your body, by going to the soul level.

This is the place for meditation. A sacred opening in the heart as a state of being requires evolution through gradual growth. As you become a frequent resident in the temple of your heart, you become more profoundly familiar with prayer than you are with fear or worry. Prayer is direct communication—verbal or non-verbal—with God. As you meditate with this level of connection, you build spiritual stamina. The layers of suffering melt off you without you ever knowing how heavy they were. One split second of being Divinely touched in the awe of this connection has the power to heal lifetimes of struggle you might carry.

Experiencing the heart's center leaves you speechless. Enjoy the silence and the clarity of your breath as you source yourself with spiritual strength for Life.

The Experience of the Ecstatic Heart

A spiritually open heart in Contemplative Being lends itself to the experience of the ecstatic heart (called "ananda," in yoga). As prana (life-force energy or Grace) enters the heart, it ignites the elevated powers of the Heart Chakra, which are Love, Bliss, Joy, Elation, Ecstasy, and Gratitude. This state can be reached through consistent meditation, dance, and also devotional music or chanting. Musical, tonal, or fluid experiences of the body merging with the flow of Grace are what move the spirit into the proper alignment that make the ecstatic heart come alive in us. It is an experience of consciousness, not a mental one.

The mind (or Ego) can and does block the elevated states of the Heart Chakra. We can easily talk ourselves out of a good thing, or get nervous if life is too good. How many times in your life, for instance, have you stopped yourself from feeling joy? Have you ever felt blissful or elated? Have you ever felt so in love with life that you felt connected to God and all beings? Can you also recall times when you might have stopped yourself from feeling joy, bliss, elation, and love because you were too afraid to let yourself feel such intense feelings?

Many of us did not grow up in environments that supported our being in the higher power of the Heart Chakra, and yet, our soul yearns to be in the true state of happiness that occurs in the experience of the ecstatic heart. The ecstatic heart is a manifestation of Divine union, between Soul and Source, felt in the body. It is a vibrational experience, which is why it can be felt through music, chanting, breathing, and devotional practices that bypass the mind and go directly to body-felt experiences.

A signature aspect of the stage of Contemplative Being is the capacity to live fully our light *and* embrace our shadow, or "darker," side. Engaging our entire experience means living fully, in truth. Stepping into our full potential, we make a powerful commitment to live the life that is our birthright. Once we reach the stage of Contemplative Being, we are familiar with the experience of living out of union with the Divine, and we know that living entirely from the Ego is not only responsible for spiritual disconnect, but also that it will never bring us the heart-connected life of fulfillment for which our soul yearns. Having endured the unfulfilled, disconnected life, we stepped out of the suffering of our wounds, connected to the power of our soul, and committed to healing, wholeness, and living from and through our light. In our healing process, we became adept enough at managing emotional experiences to empower ourselves. We passed through the depths of our experiences fully awake, and then equally awake, we soared to the heights of pure joy and divine love.

Arriving thus, at the stage of Contemplative Being, we know:

- ♥ Courage because we overcame hardship.
- ♥ Humility because we experienced humiliation.
- ♥ Love because we experienced loss.
- ♥ Forgiveness because we long to be free.
- ♥ Joy because we rose up from suppression.
- ♥ How to stay centered because we walked through anger to claim our power.
- ♥ Peace because in Chaos, we had to surrender our wounded ego.

♥ Acceptance because the pain of resistance eventually brought the words "I accept" to our lips.

♥ Truth because to live crooked hurts ourselves and others.

♥ We have healed because our relationship to our emotions is transformed.

Purpose and Meaning

In Contemplative Being, we embody the power of the highest states of the heart chakra: elation, joy, happiness, love, and bliss. We sit fully in the center of our being, empowered and divinely connected. From this place, our heart naturally connects us to the desire to share our gifts with the world, to be of service. *How*, you may wonder, *will I be the unique expression of my light in the world*? This is a question we might ask throughout our entire lives, but it is in the stage of Contemplative Being, where we live on purpose and with meaning, that we have the best chance of finding an answer that makes sense to us. When the question of purpose comes before the stage of Contemplative Being, the path of Purpose can wind like a river through the landscape of our lives because purpose is not about doing. Purpose is about understanding our light and how to be that light in the world. If you have not yet processed your old grief, anger, resentment, fears, or shame, then how will you feel your true light? Who are you without all that baggage? Do you know who you are? Have you over-identified with your old baggage? Have you met yourself in your light? How can you be purposeful if your shadow eclipses your light?

If you are seeking true Purpose in life, it is necessary to know your true Self. Are you afraid of being your light? Are you afraid of love? Do you choose the familiarity of sadness over the experience of joy? Many people do! To know the light of your true Self is a journey you take into truth. You can't flip a switch and turn the light on. You have to shift gradually and let yourself get comfortable with each new state of being; your behaviors and ways of being have to acclimate to each change you bring into your life through healing. The more you feel at home living from your true Self, the more you will know that *your Purpose is to be of service to your light.* From there, whatever you choose to *do* in life to express that light is an expression of your free will, but it is not your purpose, strictly speaking.

Know your light! What does your light look like and feel like? If you cannot feel that, then blocks remain to clear. It is necessary to go back to the Stage of Healing to understand how to identify and process emotions. Otherwise, to try to feel your light with anger, grief, or fear in your system will just throw you back into the story of your past. A multitude of reasons will always exist for why you think you can't feel your light, including people and experiences to blame, and past wounds that keep you triggered. It is your powerful Self, however, that is directing you toward healing as it shines your light on shadow places in your system, unmasking vulnerabilities and creating openings for healing to take place. In these moments, it is important to go back to the Stage of Healing and work on the emotions that come up for you—when you feel vulnerable, when you want to blame others, and when you are triggered.

Why Faith Matters

People who come to me for spiritual healing often express a desire to live a meaningful, purposeful life, but they feel stuck, alienated, and disconnected. From their place of disconnect, they seek outside psychics, books, or the opinions of friends and loved ones to help them figure out what they should *do* in life to find purpose and meaning, often unsuccessfully. The problem is not that they are stuck; nor is it problematic that they cannot connect to purpose. The difficulty in their approach comes from a lack of awareness in the potential of Divine Source. When we go outside of ourselves to find answers to life's questions, we are not connecting to a source that will bring us the answers we want and need. I know full well that intuition, gut feelings, perseverance, and willpower can bring anyone through challenging times. But there's more to life than just getting through the hard times. Even individuals who have overcome enormous obstacles in life still long for something more. The more we seek, the more what we want comes to us when we access faith, thereby making ourselves available for the heart-opening experiences that bring us through healing to the light of our soul's meaning and purpose.

Finding Purpose Can Lead You into Heartbreak

I once worked with a woman who came to me for spiritual support because she deeply wanted to find her purpose and meaning in life. She told me she'd met a man through a very magical experience, and she wanted to know whether he would be in a long-term relationship with her. I did not know because although the Divine was at work, she had personal choice, so the future was not predictable (*which is why it's so important to develop your own intuitive sense of self.*) The fate of the relationship was really up to her, not me, but it looked very promising, and I encouraged her to go forward with it and see how it went. At the same time, we were discussing that her heart needed some support since it was closed and not allowing her to feel its desires.

After a number of months, this woman remained undecided about the relationship's viability and decided to end it. She told me she was angry with me because she had felt led into the relationship experience, and she had never let a man in so deeply before. She was forty-five years old and had never had a long-term relationship, but she longed for one. She requested to have a heart opening so she could find her purpose in life. If the heart is closed down, life experiences will present themselves to break the heart open. It does not matter whether it is heartbreak with a romantic partner, or a job, or the loss of a loved one. If the soul has made a clear decision to go forward, it will. Consciously, she needed to know that going forward did not mean it would be smooth sailing. A heartbreak is the heart breaking open to get to the tender soul on the inside. It may not make the emotions feel any better, but after knowing that the big picture entails progress, she could simply let herself feel her feelings: cry, throw pillows, yell in her car, or do whatever she needed to work through the emotion that arose in the moment. I realize that I can't help everyone, but I gave her the tools to work with. I don't know what became of her, but I pray for her heart expansion and happiness.

Emotional Intimacy with the Divine

Purpose and meaning in life can be translated as having positive emotional intimacy with the Divine in every one of life's experiences—not just some experiences, but all of them. This intimacy means we stick to our firm commitment that no matter what struggles life presents, we welcome the difficult emotions with gratitude because they help us grow and make us stronger. When we emerge from the petty details of struggles and challenges, taking a bird's-eye view, we can look down on ourselves and laugh. In this way, we become spectators of the lives we are living, applauding ourselves as audience members watching an award-winning performance in which we play the starring role. From this perspective, it's also easy to see how overly dramatic and ridiculous we sometimes can be.

Emotional intimacy with the Divine can be a somatic and non-verbal experience in the body. It is a heartfelt experience and a practice. Guided meditations and visualizations are what help me to practice emotional intimacy with the Divine. Below is a meditation to guide you through the sensation of the Divine moving through your body.

You can also access an audio version of this meditation through my website: www.SchoolofIntuitiveStudies.com.

Close your eyes and visualize the most beautiful, angelic, brilliant gold and white light pouring into the crown of your head and washing your mind clear of distracting thoughts.

The light comes in to help release thoughts, by relaxing your headspace. The light continues down through your throat and relaxes your shoulders. Your shoulder blades slide down your back and your heart lifts.

A breath comes. Your breath becomes more potent. The light enters your heart very softly. There may be a sensation of emotion or resistance. Whatever it is, it is the energy between your soul and this flow of Grace. So breathe, cry if you need to, and maybe feel embarrassed or humiliated; your jaw may tighten, but you breathe with such patience through the resistance.... Keep breathing....

Eventually, the resistance softens and you have a sensation that you are connected through this pipeline between the Divine and your Self.

Will this feeling persist? Well, with practice and commitment, it will. In fact, allowing this energy into your body will raise your consciousness to such a degree that it makes it easier for you to make different choices in your life. It is not that life will be giving you more because you visualize this, but because you choose to transform this relationship into feeling a higher frequency of love, a shift can come. Assuming the responsibility for creating life the way you want it to be, you see the good in others, attract healthy people into your life, live a harmonious lifestyle, etc. These are not things you have to go out and find. These are manifestations of the heart being sourced by Divine Grace.

Is Contemplative Being an Easy Stage?

Sometimes it is and sometimes it isn't. It has its own challenges of being alive to more pain in the world, where previously you may have been numb to it. Yet, in Contemplative Being, you both cry for the grievances of the world and you laugh when true spirit shines through. What becomes easier in Contemplative Being is that you remember your spiritual sourcing as a waking practice, and you know you are not alone. Therefore, the wounded ego is less powerful, and you handle life with more grace, love, empowerment, vulnerability, truth, forgiveness, and integrity.

Don't feel bad if you're not here yet, and if Contemplative Being isn't resonating with you. There is nothing wrong with you. Have compassion for where you are. Healing can take a while. The Healing Guide is there for you to return to as often as you need it, so it may serve you to go back to the healing guide or anywhere in this book to support yourself through that stage.

My prayer for you is that this book provides a guideline for you to understand you are a powerful being on this earth and you are here on purpose. May you see your journey through a spiritual lens and may the Divine be a part of your daily life. You are neither your wounds, nor your story. You are a spiritually progressing soul, and as such, you always have the ability to transform your past and become who you are here to be.

REFLECTION QUESTIONS

I have a dear friend who, whenever she called me, would not ask me, "How are you?" but "How's your heart?" So I pass the question on to you after going through an Initial Heart Opening, Chaos, and Healing:

How is your heart?

What have you learned about who you are?

What are you continuing to learn?

What life changes have you made for the better?

What have you let go of, and what are you having more of?

How do you now daily Source yourself?

What is your relationship to your intuition?

What do you need in your life to maintain your continued emotional, personal, and spiritual growth?

What is your purpose right now? Not forever, but in this moment?

What does the word Love mean to you now?

What is your relationship to Love now? Do you let it in? How?

What does living from a spiritually open heart mean to you?

What does Heart Consciousness mean to you?

♫ **GUIDED MEDITATION AUDIO**

Log in to www.SchoolofIntuitiveStudies.com through the Expanding Your Heart link to receive your guided meditation titled "Contemplative Being Meditation."

A Final Note:
EXPANDING *YOUR* HEART

Now that you have read this book, how are you going to live your Expanded Heart in the world? Years ago, society didn't support living your truth, heart, and light in the world, so it was scary to do so. Perhaps you were shamed, criticized, or hurt in just speaking your truth or being who you are. Times have changed. People are becoming more aware, conscious, and going for it. Now, you are being *called* to live more courageously with your Expanded Heart in the world.

How are you going to do this? How are you going to let go of the past so that not only your mind, but your energy is living more in the present moment with your light? How are you no longer going to fear your light? Or how are you no longer going to fear love? How will the paradigm shift in *you* so your system is updated to the changes happening rapidly on this globe? The universe is asking all beings to step more fully into their expansion of self and of heart. How will do you this?

This book's content is intended to support you in your journey of healing and expanding your heart. It doesn't work, however, if you read the book and don't apply the tools. While reading this book, did you bookmark any pages that you need to come back to so you can do a piece of self-work? Did you think "Oh, I really need to do that, but that's a bit scary," or "I'll do it later"? I'm asking you to take some action. Think about ten things you can do to help yourself through the Four Stages, or to help you be more successful in living your light and expanded heart in the world.

List ten things you *will* do:

1. _____

2. _____

3. _____

4. _____

5. _____

6. _____

7. _____

8. _____

9. _____

10. _____

In this book, you have learned that the challenges you have been through can be doorways to opening your spiritual heart. The doorway may not open from the difficulty itself, but from the healing that results from the challenges. You've learned about the role chaos plays and how to move through your healing process. Part of succeeding in your healing requires asking for help, knowing you are not alone, and building connection or community to support you in your process. "I get by with a little help from my friends," right? Everyone needs support during his or her deepest transformation, growth, and healing. If you find you cannot do it alone, you are *normal*. Everyone has something to offer that can give another a gift of growth. *You* have something to offer from your life experience that may just be the advice a person needs to hear.

I realize your greatness, and I also realize you may need support to see that greatness. I have created resources for you to connect with others like you, through book clubs, workshops, and trainings. I'm happy to give you more resources and direction on your healing. You can come over to my website: www.SchoolofIntuitiveStudies.com.

I wish you the best of everything and send you many blessings on your path to Expanding Your Heart.

Blessings,

Wendy DeRosa

ABOUT THE AUTHOR

WENDY DE ROSA is an author, professional keynote speaker, teacher, and a national and international intuitive energy healer. Since 1998, Wendy has worked with people all over the world, using her intuitive gifts to help thousands enrich their lives, clear energy blocks, and discover their deeper selves. She offers online and in-person classes in intuitive energy healing and developing intuition. Her programs provide extensive education for spiritual growth and a personal process for any person wanting to expand his or her skills, connect to the Divine, and experience personal transformation.

Wendy is the founder of The School of Intuitive Studies and The Healer Training Program where she trains healers and non-healers with interest in self-healing. The Healer Training Program ran in four different cities in the U.S. before becoming the first online training of its kind. The Healer Training Program now runs exclusively online under Wendy's personal facilitating.

Wendy appeared on CBS News/*Better Connecticut* four times in 2013 and 2014, offering education on the importance of intuition in daily life. Wendy's book *Energy Healing Through the Chakras: A Guide to*

Self-Healing is an Amazon Best-Seller and available on Amazon.com. Wendy has also published articles, and she is a contributing author to the best-selling book, *Bouncing Back: Thriving in Changing Times* with such fellow leaders in personal growth as Wayne Dyer, Bryan Tracy, and John Assaraf.

Since 2004, Wendy has offered a Free Conference Call Healing every third Tuesday of the month for people across the globe to experience energy healing. Aware that not everyone can afford energy healing, this call has been Wendy's service offering to the worldwide community. Anyone anywhere is welcome to participate in a FREE healing. Details are available through Wendy's email list and on her website.

Although, a bit of a global citizen, Wendy lives an ever-expanding life with her husband, daughter, and stepson in Boulder, Colorado. She enjoys being with her family, practicing yoga, traveling, teaching, writing, exploring the outdoors, and being a student of life.

For more information, visit:
www.SchoolofIntuitiveStudies.com

INTUITIVE HEALER TRAINING PROGRAM

Are you intuitive? Are you ready to shed layers so your soul can shine?

Would you like to work with me—Wendy—personally, learn how to develop your intuitive gifts, and heal the blocks to your heart expansion? If so, I'd love to introduce you to my signature program, The "Intuitive" Healer Training Program, where I can take you deeper into your healing process.

The Intuitive Healer Training Program is an in-depth personal growth program that gives you training in energy healing, developing your intuition, and living more Divinely connected.

This program is for you if you're a therapist, coach, practitioner, teacher, parent, or just interested in developing your intuition and personal healing and stepping into the power of who you are meant to be.

You don't have to want to be a healer to participate in this program. You just have to want personal expansion, spiritual growth, and in-depth and experiential learning of intuition.

What is a healer anyway?

A healer administers personal transformation.

So if you want to transform any aspect of your life, begin to live in an empowered way, and empower others, then there is a healer ability within you to help yourself...and **this course is for you.**

In this groundbreaking program, you will deepen your intuition while clearing your blocks through energy healing, leaving you fully equipped to affect total personal transformation for yourself and/or for others.

All About the Intuitive Healer Training Program

You will acquire the skills to administer transformation for yourself and for others. More importantly, you will heal lifelong energy blocks to living your true light in the world. This program is the most in-depth, evolutionary, supportive, and powerful training and certification course of its kind.

Learning Objectives:

- ♥ Enable yourself to let go and unravel the blocks that have been keeping you small.
- ♥ Find the center of your *true* self—not who you were conditioned to be.
- ♥ Discover that your intuitive gifts are strengths, not weaknesses.
- ♥ Learn how to live your gifts in an empowered, clear, and grounded way.
- ♥ Separate true, meaningful intuition from mental chatter.
- ♥ Facilitate healing for yourself and for others.
- ♥ Tap into the power within, instead of looking outward for answers.

♥ Live life Divinely connected, instead of feeling disconnected, empty, or longing.

You will learn how intuition works in the body, what are the four different types of intuition, what power centers they come from in your body, and how to access them. Learning how these abilities work does *not* make you a metaphysical odd bird. Understanding them makes you *whole* because you cease suppressing natural ways that your spirit takes in information from life.

So if you feel ready to be nurtured, guided, and held in a process of expanding your intuitive gifts and healing abilities, you are ready for the Intuitive Healer Training Program.

Visit: www.SchoolofIntuitiveStudies.com

Join the Movement!
THE EXPANDING YOUR HEART BOOK CLUB

A movement is happening and you are invited to hop on board! People everywhere are experiencing Heart Expansions, whether they realize it or not. Because this process can be intense at times or people need support, I have created the **Expanding Your Heart Book Club**.

When reading this book, you may have gotten in touch with your story more deeply. You may have experienced one, two, or all Four Stages of a Spiritual Opening. These book clubs are opportunities for you to work together with others in your community to discuss the book, share ideas and experiences, offer suggestions for energy healing tools, and create healthy bonding.

The book clubs are led in-person and virtually all over the world by myself, a Held in Light Healer or facilitator with knowledge of the Divine healing. These books clubs are not a place to complain, control, or keep a victim story going. These clubs are a chance for you to connect more to your spiritual light and the *true you*, through the context of the book. The facilitators are trained to guide the group and you to connecting to your true light.

If you would like to find a book club near you or virtually, please visit: www.SchoolofIntuitiveStudies.com.

Book Club Guidelines

Book clubs are a wonderful way for people to come together to talk about a book. Friendships are made, ideas are shared, and growth happens when people gather to learn something new. This book is a roadmap for your personal healing and life journey. Many people share similar experiences, and it can be a lonely journey if you are not aware that others have been in your shoes. Being in a group around this book in particular can be an incredibly supportive, empowering, heart opening, and healing process. To ensure a successful book club experience, I ask that you review and agree to the Expanding Your Heart Book Club Code of Ethics below.

Expanding Your Heart Book Club Code of Ethics

- ♥ Create a listening, sharing, and supportive environment for your Book Club group.
- ♥ Create a safe, trusting, non-judgmental, and honest environment for the group, and ask your participants to do the same for the group.
- ♥ Invite people who share the desire to grow, heal, evolve, and learn.
- ♥ Personality characteristics such as negativity, victimizing, or being critical, judgmental, or harmful may be attached to people who may not be a fit for your book club. Check in with your intuition on who feels like a fit for you.
- ♥ Know that groups can be triggering for people, but that's okay! Breathe and stay honest with yourself on *your* stuff, rather than

making another person wrong.

♥ Respect and honor the confidentiality of individuals' personal experiences discussed in the group.

♥ When sharing, set a timer, allowing each person to have five to seven minutes to share his or her experience, followed by ten to fifteen minutes for group support if needed. Use your own discretion if more time is needed per person. Timing may vary depending on the number of people in the group.

♥ Respectfully listen to and share with others in your group.

♥ When offering feedback or support, be careful not to project your experience onto someone in the group. For example, if someone is struggling with sending her child off to school, and you had that same experience years prior, but you didn't have a struggle, don't assume she can move through it the way you did. Everyone comes with a different backdrop to every life experience. Typically, the issue is not the present experience. Instead, it is the backdrop that is coming to the foreground. Hold space, listen, and allow each person to share.

♥ Be careful not to tell people "You should do this," or "You know what you should do." If someone asks for group support, then you can offer your two cents. Otherwise, listening with compassion is sometimes the best support you can offer.

♥ My strong recommendation is that alcohol not be offered when discussing the Four Stages in a book club setting. Consuming alcohol makes it very hard to keep clear boundaries, which could lead to participants taking on issues that might be beyond the scope of the group and this book's content. This situation has the potential to open up messy process work that would be challenging to clear up, leaving participants exposed and vulnerable. I do not recommend consuming alcohol or any recreational drugs when moving through the content of this material.

Please note: Your friends and colleagues may not be therapists or practitioners, and even if they are, they may not be available to support you fully through an issue that may come up for you. If, in the course of a group process experience, you feel you are going through or processing more than what your peers can hold, I recommend you seek outside support to help you move through your issue. I also recommend that the group boundaries be clear, confidential (if necessary), and that group members not be afraid to encourage participants to seek support outside the group if necessary.

My prayer is that this book will provide a resource for your empowerment and spiritual growth, and for you to expand your heart consciousness so you can hear all the ways the Divine is calling you home to yourself.

BOOK WENDY DE ROSA
TO SPEAK AT YOUR NEXT EVENT

You are in for an inspirational, healing, and transformational treat by booking Wendy De Rosa for your next event. Wendy doesn't just deliver a talk. She delivers an *experience*. Wendy's words and presence are infused with healing, light, and empowerment. The audience receives a healing and leaves feeling inspired to make changes.

Whether it's an audience of 10 or 10,000, Wendy calibrates to the collective energy of the room and speaks directly to the hearts of everyone present. The teachings and healings are so personal that it feels like She wrote a speech just for you. She is a present, strong, clear, and personable facilitator. She combines humor, intensity, heart, and personality in her delivery, which makes her infectious and loveable. Your audience members leave feeling seen and that they have a purpose.

Wendy is available for speaking in the U.S and abroad. She is also available to facilitate book club events and workshops virtually and in-person.

To book Wendy at your next event, contact:

Wendy De Rosa
www.SchoolofIntuitiveStudies.com
Info@SchoolofIntuitiveStudies.com